Crochet Designs for the Home

20 Elegant Patterns
From the Archives of
DMC

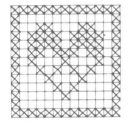 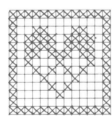 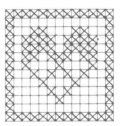

Dover Publications, Inc.

New York

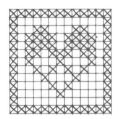

Published in Canada by General Publishing Company, Ltd., 30 Lesmill Road, Don Mills, Toronto, Ontario.
Published in the United Kingdom by Constable and Company, Ltd., 10 Orange Street, London WC2H 7EG.

Crochet Designs for the Home: 20 Elegant Patterns From the Archives of DMC, first published by Dover Publications, Inc., in 1990, is a selection of 20 patterns originally published by Dollfus-Mieg & Co, AS, Copenhagen, Denmark.

Manufactured in the United States of America
Dover Publications, Inc., 31 East 2nd Street, Mineola, N.Y. 11501

Library of Congress Cataloging-in-Publication Data

Crochet designs for the home : 20 elegant patterns from the archives of DMC.
          p.   cm.
    ISBN 0-486-26168-9
    1. Crocheting—Patterns.   I. Dollfus-Mieg & Cie.
TT820.C873   1990
746.43′4041—dc20   89-25738
                                                         CIP

Introduction

Dollfus-Mieg & Co. AS, better known as DMC, is one of the oldest, largest and most respected firms in the needlework industry, with branches in various countries around the world. Not only is DMC known for the variety and high quality of the threads they produce, but also for their innovative and creative designs in all areas of needlework.

In needlework design, Europeans have a style and elegance all their own. Fine crocheted lace, particularly, is a European tradition, one that American crocheters have come to admire. For this book, the Danish branch of DMC has selected twenty of their finest patterns for doilies, tablecloths, runners and more, to give your home a Continental flavor.

How to Crochet

Slip Knot

Grasp the loose end of the thread with your left hand and make an "O" with the thread leading from the ball (the ball of thread should be hanging behind the "O"). Pinch the top of the "O" between the thumb and middle finger of your left hand, and hold your crochet hook in your right hand as you would hold a pencil. Insert the tip of the hook and bring a loop from the thread ball through the "O" (*Fig. 1*). Tighten the loop to complete the slip knot (*Fig. 2*). You are now ready to make your first chain stitch (remember that the loop on your hook never counts when you are counting the stitches in your work).

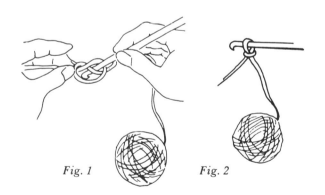

Fig. 1   Fig. 2

Chain Stitch

Pinch the base of the slip knot between the thumb and middle finger of your left hand, and wind the thread from the ball from back to front over your forefinger. With the crochet hook inserted in the slip knot and the tip of the hook curved toward you, wrap the thread around the hook from back to front (*Fig. 3*)—this is called a yarn-over. Pull the thread through the loop on the hook to complete the first chain stitch. Yarn-over again and pull through the loop on

the hook the number of times specified (*Fig. 4*). Each chain (and later each single crochet or other stitch) forms a distinct oval that can be clearly seen from the top of the work.

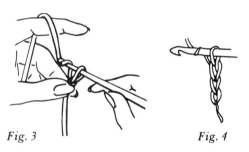

Fig. 3   Fig. 4

Counting the Chain Stitches: Just as a slip knot must be placed on the hook in the beginning, there must always be a loop on the hook before starting a new stitch. The loop on the hook is considered the beginning of each succeeding stitch and, therefore, does not count as a stitch. In a row of chain stitches, the chain stitch next to the loop on the hook is counted as the first stitch from the hook, the chain stitch preceding that one is the second stitch from the hook, and so on (*Fig. 5*).

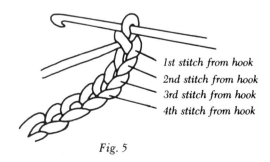

1st stitch from hook
2nd stitch from hook
3rd stitch from hook
4th stitch from hook

Fig. 5

Single Crochet

Make a foundation chain of the required number of stitches (remember that the loop on the hook does not count as a stitch and that, for single crochet, you will need one chain for each stitch you want to make plus one additional chain for turning). Keeping the thread from the ball wrapped from back to front over your left forefinger, begin the first single crochet stitch by inserting the hook from front to back in the second chain from the hook, taking care to push the hook through the center of the oval (*Fig. 6*). Then yarn-over—that is, bring the thread over the hook from back to front (*Fig. 7*)—and pull the thread through the stitch. You now have two loops on the hook (*Fig. 8*). Yarn-over again (*Fig. 9*) and pull the thread through both loops on the hook to complete the first single crochet stitch (*Fig. 10*). You now have only one loop left on the hook and are ready to begin

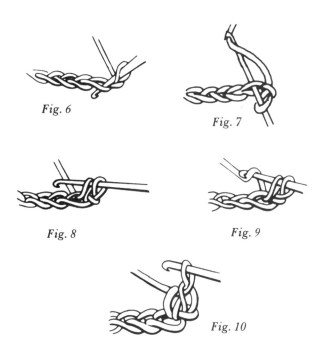

Fig. 6
Fig. 7
Fig. 8
Fig. 9
Fig. 10

the next stitch. Repeat the procedure until you have worked one single crochet stitch in each stitch of the foundation chain. Unless the pattern instructions specify otherwise, at the end of the first row and of each succeeding single crochet row, make one chain stitch (*Fig. 11*) and then turn the work so the thread from the ball is once again at the right edge. For succeeding rows of single crochet, unless the pattern instructions specifically tell you to do otherwise, always make the first stitch of a row in the last single crochet stitch of the previous row (that is, in the second stitch from the hook), not in the turning chain; and work each stitch by inserting the hook under both strands that form the oval of the stitch of the previous row (*Fig. 12*).

Fig. 11
Fig. 12

Half Double Crochet

Make a foundation chain of the required number of stitches (remember that the loop on the hook does not count as a stitch and that, for half double crochet, you will need one chain for each stitch you want to make plus two additional chains for turning). To begin the first half double crochet stitch, first make sure that the thread from the ball is wrapped from back to front over your left forefinger. Then yarn-over (bring the thread over the hook from back to front) (*Fig. 13*) and insert the hook from front to back in the third chain from the hook, taking care to push the hook through the center of the oval. Yarn-over again and pull the thread through the stitch. You now have three loops on the hook (*Fig. 14*). Yarn-over once more and pull the thread through all three loops on the hook to complete the first half double crochet stitch (*Fig. 15*). You now have only one loop left on the hook and are ready to begin the next stitch. Repeat the procedure until you have worked one half double crochet stitch in each stitch of the foundation chain. Unless the pattern instructions specify otherwise, at the end of the first row and of each succeeding half double crochet row, make two chain stitches and then turn the work so the thread from the ball is once again at the right edge. For succeeding rows of half double crochet, unless the instructions specifically tell you to do otherwise, always make the first stitch of a row in the last half double crochet stitch of the previous row (that is, in the third stitch from the hook), not in the turning chain; and work each stitch by inserting the hook under both strands that form the oval of the stitch of the previous row.

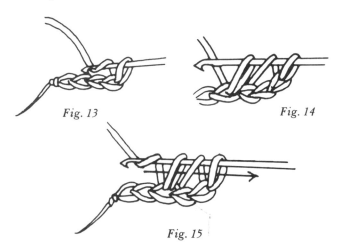

Fig. 13
Fig. 14
Fig. 15

Double Crochet

Make a foundation chain of the required number of stitches (remember that the loop on the hook does not count as a stitch and that, for double crochet, you will need one chain for each stitch you want to make plus three additional chains for turning). To begin the first double crochet stitch, first make sure that the thread from the ball is wrapped from back to front over your left forefinger. Then yarn-over (bring the thread over the hook from back to front) (*Fig. 16*); and insert the hook from front to back in the fourth chain from the hook, taking care to push the hook through the center of the oval. Yarn-over again and pull the thread through the stitch. You now have three loops on the hook (*Fig. 17*). Yarn-over again and pull the thread through the first two loops on the hook. You now have two loops left on

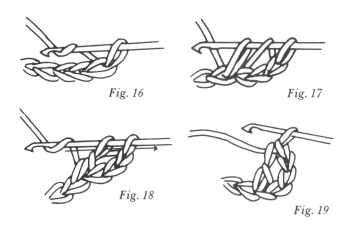

Fig. 16

Fig. 17

Fig. 18

Fig. 19

the hook; yarn-over once more and pull the thread through both of the loops on the hook to complete the first double crochet stitch (*Fig. 18*). You now have only one loop left on the hook and are ready to begin the next stitch (*Fig. 19*). Repeat the procedure until you have worked one double crochet stitch in each stitch of the foundation chain. Unless the pattern instructions specify otherwise, at the end of the first row and of each succeeding double crochet row, make three chain stitches and then turn the work so the thread from the ball is once again at the right edge. For succeeding rows of double crochet, unless the instructions specifically tell you to do otherwise, always make the first stitch of a row in the next to the last double crochet stitch of the previous row (the turning chain will count as one double crochet stitch); work each stitch by inserting the hook under both strands that form the oval of the stitch of the previous row.

Triple Crochet

Make a foundation chain of the required number of stitches (remember that the loop on the hook does not count as a stitch and that, for triple crochet, you will need one chain for each stitch you want to make plus four additional chains for turning). To begin the first triple crochet stitch, first make sure that the thread from the ball is wrapped from back to front over your left forefinger. Then yarn-over (bring the thread over the hook from back to front) twice (*Fig. 20*) and insert the hook from front to back in the fifth chain from the hook, taking care to push the hook through

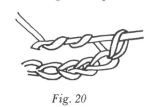

Fig. 20

Fig. 21

the center of the oval. Yarn-over again and pull the thread through the stitch (*Fig. 21*). You now have four loops on the hook. Yarn-over again and pull the thread through the first

two loops on the hook. You now have three loops left on the hook. Yarn-over again and pull the thread through the next two loops on the hook. You now have two loops on the hook; yarn-over once more and pull the thread through both the loops on the hook to complete the first triple crochet stitch. You now have only one loop left on the hook and are ready to begin the next stitch. Repeat the procedure until you have worked one triple crochet stitch in each stitch of the foundation chain. Unless the pattern instructions specify otherwise, at the end of the first row and of each succeeding triple crochet row, make four chain stitches and then turn the work so that the thread from the ball is once again at the right edge. For succeeding rows of triple crochet, unless the instructions specifically tell you to do otherwise, always make the first stitch of a row in the next to the last triple crochet stitch of the previous row (the turning chain will count as one triple crochet stitch) and work each stitch by inserting the hook under both strands that form the oval of the stitch of the previous row.

Double Treble Crochet

Make a foundation chain of the required number of stitches (remember that the loop on the hook does not count as a stitch and that, for double treble crochet, you will need one chain for each stitch you want to make plus five additional chains for turning). To begin the first double treble crochet stitch, first make sure that the thread from the ball is wrapped from back to front over your left forefinger. Then yarn-over (bring the thread over the hook from back to front) three times (*Fig. 22*) and insert the hook from front to

Fig. 22

back in the sixth chain from the hook, taking care to push the hook through the center of the oval. Yarn-over again and pull the thread through the stitch. You now have five loops on the hook. Yarn-over again and pull the thread through the first two loops on the hook. You now have four loops left on the hook. Yarn-over again and pull the thread through the next two loops on the hook. You now have three loops on the hook. Yarn-over again and pull the thread through the next two loops on the hook. You now have two loops on the hook; yarn-over once more and pull the thread through both the loops on the hook to complete the first double treble crochet stitch. You now have only one loop left on the hook and are ready to begin the next stitch. Repeat the procedure until you have worked one double treble crochet stitch in each stitch of the foundation chain. Unless the pattern instructions specify otherwise, at the end of the first row and of each succeeding double treble crochet row, make five chain stitches and then turn the work so that the thread from the ball is once again at the right edge. For succeeding rows of double treble crochet, unless the instructions specifically tell you to do otherwise, always make the first stitch of a row in the next to the last double treble crochet stitch of the previous row (the turning chain will count as one double treble crochet stitch) and work each stitch by inserting the hook under both strands that form the oval of the stitch of the previous row.

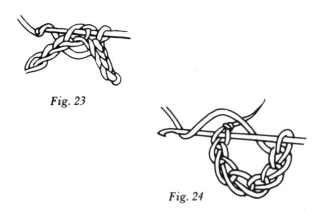

Fig. 23

Fig. 24

Slip Stitch

Insert the hook in a stitch, yarn-over and then pull the thread through both the stitch and the loop on the hook in one motion (*Fig. 23*). Slip stitch is similar to single crochet, but you do not yarn-over a second time before pulling the thread through the loop on the hook. It is an important utility stitch and is used, for example, to join the ends of a foundation chain to form a ring (*Fig. 24*), to smoothly finish the edge of a piece worked in rounds and to work across an edge without adding appreciable height to the piece.

Working in a Chain Space

A series of chain stitches is often used to bridge an open space—as, for example, when working a lacelike design. To crochet the next row or round, the pattern instructions may tell you to work across the "bridge" of chain stitches by working a given type and number of stitches in the chain space rather than into the chain stitches themselves. This means that, in order to make each of the stitches in question, you must insert the hook from front to back into the space below the chain (*Fig. 25*) and then work the stitch around the chain (*Fig. 26*).

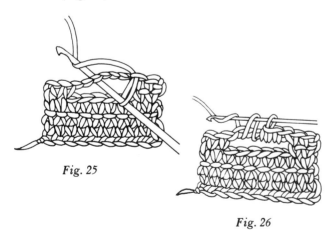

Fig. 25

Fig. 26

Increasing and Decreasing

To increase one stitch, work two stitches in the same stitch of the previous row; or work a stitch in the turning chain at the beginning or end of a row. Pattern instructions will specify which method to use.

To decrease one stitch, work two stitches together in the following way: work the first stitch until the final yarn-over, but do not yarn-over; instead, begin to work the next stitch, working it also to the final yarn-over. Now yarn-over and pull the thread through all the loops on the hook.

Attaching New Thread

If you run out of thread in the course of working a piece, complete a stitch with the old thread; then hold the new thread against the back (wrong side) of the work, leaving a loose 4″ end. Insert the hook into the next stitch to be worked, yarn-over and draw a loop of the new thread through the stitch. Finish the stitch and continue working in the usual manner, using the new thread.

When you must attach new thread along the edge of a completed piece in order to work an edging or the first row of another section of the project, hold the new thread against the back of the work, leaving a 4″ end. Insert the hook into the stitch in which the thread is to be attached, yarn-over and draw a loop through the stitch; then chain one. You are now ready to pick up and work the number of stitches specified in the instructions. Hold the thread end along the edge of the piece and work it into the first few stitches or, if you prefer, let it hang at the back of the piece and weave it in later.

Ending Off

Complete the last stitch of the piece and cut the thread from the ball, leaving a 4″ thread end (or a thread end of the length specified in the instructions). Then draw the thread end through the remaining loop on the hook and pull tight. Thread the end on a large-eyed yarn needle and, unless the project directions tell you to do otherwise, weave the thread end through the back of the work for about 1″ and trim the excess.

Blocking

After you have completed your project, you should wash and block it. If the piece is made up of separate motifs sewn together, you may find it easier to block the motifs before you join them.

Using a mild soap and cool water, squeeze the suds gently through the crochet; do not rub. Rinse the piece thoroughly. If desired, lightly starch small pieces such as doilies and placemats. Using rustproof pins, pin the piece right side down on a well-padded surface, pinning each picot and loop in place. When the crochet is almost dry, press it through a damp cloth with a moderately hot iron. Do not allow the iron to rest on the stitches.

Gauge

Most of the patterns in this book include a *gauge*, telling you how many stitches you should have per inch, or how large a motif should be after a certain number of rounds. If you do not work to the proper gauge, your piece will not be the size listed in the instructions.

Before beginning any project, work a small sample using the thread and crochet hook called for. If your sample is larger than specified by the gauge, use a smaller hook; if smaller, use a larger hook.

Abbreviations

beg	begin or beginning	rnd(s)	round(s)
bet	between	sc	single crochet
ch(s)	chain(s)	sp	space
ch-sp	chain-space	sl st	slip stitch
dec	decrease	st(s)	stitch(es)
dc	double crochet	tr	triple crochet
dtr	double treble crochet	tr tr	triple treble crochet (yo hook 4 times)
hdc	half double crochet		
lp(s)	loop(s)	yds	yards
rem	remain or remaining	yo	yarn-over
rep	repeat		

The terminology and hooks listed in this book are those used in the United States. The following charts give the U.S. names of crochet stitches and their equivalents in other countries and the approximate equivalents to U.S. crochet hook sizes.

STITCH CONVERSION CHART

U.S. Name	Equivalent
Chain	Chain
Slip	Single crochet
Single crochet	Double crochet
Half-double or short-double crochet	Half-treble crochet
Double crochet	Treble crochet
Treble crochet	Double-treble crochet
Double-treble crochet	Treble-treble crochet
Treble-treble or long-treble crochet	Quadruple-treble crochet
Afghan stitch	Tricot crochet

STEEL CROCHET HOOK CONVERSION CHART

U.S. Size	00	0	1	2	3	4	5	6	7	8	9	10	11	12	13	14
British & Canadian Size	000	00	0	1	–	1½	2	2½	–	3	–	4	–	5	–	6
Metric Size (mm)	3.00	2.75	2.50	2.25	2.10	2.00	1.90	1.80	1.65	1.50	1.40	1.25	1.10	1.00	0.75	0.60

Metric Conversion Chart

CONVERTING INCHES TO CENTIMETERS AND YARDS TO METERS

mm — millimeters   cm — centimeters   m — meters

INCHES INTO MILLIMETERS AND CENTIMETERS
(Slightly rounded off for convenience)

inches	mm		cm	inches	cm	inches	cm	inches	cm
⅛	3mm			5	12.5	21	53.5	38	96.5
¼	6mm			5½	14	22	56	39	99
⅜	10mm	or	1cm	6	15	23	58.5	40	101.5
½	13mm	or	1.3cm	7	18	24	61	41	104
⅝	15mm	or	1.5cm	8	20.5	25	63.5	42	106.5
¾	20mm	or	2cm	9	23	26	66	43	109
⅞	22mm	or	2.2cm	10	25.5	27	68.5	44	112
1	25mm	or	2.5cm	11	28	28	71	45	114.5
1¼	32mm	or	3.2cm	12	30.5	29	73.5	46	117
1½	38mm	or	3.8cm	13	33	30	76	47	119.5
1¾	45mm	or	4.5cm	14	35.5	31	79	48	122
2	50mm	or	5cm	15	38	32	81.5	49	124.5
2½	65mm	or	6.5cm	16	40.5	33	84	50	127
3	75mm	or	7.5cm	17	43	34	86.5		
3½	90mm	or	9cm	18	46	35	89		
4	100mm	or	10cm	19	48.5	36	91.5		
4½	115mm	or	11.5cm	20	51	37	94		

YARDS TO METERS
(Slightly rounded off for convenience)

yards	meters	yards	meters	yards	meters	yards	meters	yards	meters
⅛	0.15	2⅛	1.95	4⅛	3.80	6⅛	5.60	8⅛	7.45
¼	0.25	2¼	2.10	4¼	3.90	6¼	5.75	8¼	7.55
⅜	0.35	2⅜	2.20	4⅜	4.00	6⅜	5.85	8⅜	7.70
½	0.50	2½	2.30	4½	4.15	6½	5.95	8½	7.80
⅝	0.60	2⅝	2.40	4⅝	4.25	6⅝	6.10	8⅝	7.90
¾	0.70	2¾	2.55	4¾	4.35	6¾	6.20	8¾	8.00
⅞	0.80	2⅞	2.65	4⅞	4.50	6⅞	6.30	8⅞	8.15
1	0.95	3	2.75	5	4.60	7	6.40	9	8.25
1⅛	1.05	3⅛	2.90	5⅛	4.70	7⅛	6.55	9⅛	8.35
1¼	1.15	3¼	3.00	5¼	4.80	7¼	6.65	9¼	8.50
1⅜	1.30	3⅜	3.10	5⅜	4.95	7⅜	6.75	9⅜	8.60
1½	1.40	3½	3.20	5½	5.05	7½	6.90	9½	8.70
1⅝	1.50	3⅝	3.35	5⅝	5.15	7⅝	7.00	9⅝	8.80
1¾	1.60	3¾	3.45	5¾	5.30	7¾	7.10	9¾	8.95
1⅞	1.75	3⅞	3.55	5⅞	5.40	7⅞	7.20	9⅞	9.05
2	1.85	4	3.70	6	5.50	8	7.35	10	9.15

AVAILABLE FABRIC WIDTHS

25″	65cm	50″	127cm
27″	70cm	54″/56″	140cm
35″/36″	90cm	58″/60″	150cm
39″	100cm	68″/70″	175cm
44″/45″	115cm	72″	180cm
48″	122cm		

AVAILABLE ZIPPER LENGTHS

4″	10cm	10″	25cm	22″	55cm
5″	12cm	12″	30cm	24″	60cm
6″	15cm	14″	35cm	26″	65cm
7″	18cm	16″	40cm	28″	70cm
8″	20cm	18″	45cm	30″	75cm
9″	22cm	20″	50cm		

Golden Pansies Doily

Size: Approximately 12" in diameter.

MATERIALS

DMC Cordonnet Special, size 20—1 ball white.
DMC metallic thread—1 spool each gold #280 and silver #281.
Size 10 steel crochet hook.

Gauge: Piece should measure about 3" across after 7 rnds.

SPECIAL INSTRUCTIONS

V-st: Work dc, ch 3 and dc all in same sp.
Picot loop: Sc in sp, (ch 3, sc in 3rd ch from hook) 3 times—3 picots made, sc in same sp as last sc before picots.

CENTER

With white, ch 10, join with sl st in first ch to form ring.
Rnd 1: Ch 3, dc in ring, ch 2, *2 dc in ring, ch 2; rep from * 6 times, join with sl st in top of beg ch 3, sl st in next dc.
Rnd 2: *Sc in next ch-2 sp, ch 5; rep from * around, join in first sc, sl st in each of first 2 chs of next ch 5.

Rnd 3: Ch 3, dc in same sp, ch 3, 2 dc in same sp, ch 2, *work 2 dc, ch 3, 2 dc in next ch-sp, ch 2; rep from * around, join in top of beg ch 3.
Rnd 4: Ch 3, dc in next dc, *work V-st in next ch-3 sp, dc in each of next 2 dc, ch 2, skip ch-2 sp, dc in each of next 2 dc; rep from * around, end last rep with ch 2, join in top of beg ch 3.
Rnd 5: Ch 3, dc in each of next 2 dc, *work V-st in next ch-3 sp, dc in each of next 3 dc, ch 2, skip ch-2 sp, dc in each of next 3 dc; rep from * around, end last rep with ch 2, join in top of beg ch 3.
Rnds 6–12: Ch 3, *dc in next dc and in each dc to ch-3 sp, work V-st in ch-3 sp, dc in each dc to ch-2 sp, ch 2, skip next ch-2 sp; rep from * around, join in top of beg ch 3. You will have 11 dc in each dc group.
Rnd 13: Ch 5, *skip next 2 dc, dc in each of next 8 dc, work V-st in ch-3 sp, dc in each of next 8 dc, ch 2, skip next 2 dc, dc in last dc of group, ch 2, skip next ch-2 sp, dc in next dc, ch 2; rep from * around, end last rep with ch 2, skip next ch-2 sp, dc in 3rd ch of beg ch 5.
Rnd 14: Ch 5, skip next ch-sp, dc in next dc, *ch 2, skip

9

next 2 dc, dc in each of next 6 dc, V-st in next ch-3 sp, dc in each of next 6 dc, ch 2, skip next 2 dc, dc in next dc, (ch 2, skip next ch-2 sp, dc in next dc) 3 times; rep from * around, end last rep with ch 2, skip next ch-2 sp, join in 3rd ch of beg ch 5.

Rnd 15: Ch 5, skip next ch-sp, dc in next dc, ch 2, skip next ch-2 sp, dc in next dc, *ch 2, skip next 2 dc, dc in each of next 4 dc, V-st in next ch-3 sp, dc in each of next 4 dc, ch 2, skip next 2 dc, dc in next dc, (ch 2, skip next ch-2 sp, dc in next dc) 5 times; rep from * around, end last rep with ch 2, skip next ch-2 sp, dc in next dc, ch 2, skip next ch-2 sp, join in 3rd ch of beg ch 5.

Rnd 16: Ch 5, skip next ch-sp, dc in next dc, (ch 2, skip next ch-2 sp, dc in next dc) twice, *ch 2, skip next 2 dc, dc in each of next 2 dc, V-st in next ch-3 sp, dc in each of next 2 dc, ch 2, skip next 2 dc, dc in next dc, (ch 2, skip next ch-2 sp, dc in next dc) 7 times; rep from * around, end last rep with (ch 2, skip next ch-2 sp, dc in next dc) twice, ch 2, skip next ch-2 sp, join in 3rd ch of beg ch 5.

Rnd 17: Ch 5, skip next ch-sp, (dc in next dc, ch 2, skip next ch-2 sp) 3 times, *dc in each dc to ch-3 sp of next V-st, work dc, ch 4, dc in ch-3 sp, dc in each dc to next ch-2 sp, (ch 2, skip next ch-2 sp, dc in next dc) 9 times; rep from * around, end last rep with (ch 2, skip next ch-2 sp, dc in next dc) 4 times, ch 2, skip next ch-2 sp, join in 3rd ch of beg ch 5.

Rnds 18–20: Ch 5, skip next ch-sp, (dc in next dc, ch 2, skip next ch-2 sp) 3 times, *dc in each dc to next ch-4 sp, work dc, ch 4, dc in ch-4 sp, dc in each dc to next ch-2 sp, (ch 2, skip next ch-2 sp, dc in next dc) 9 times; rep from * around, end last rep with (ch 2, skip next ch-2 sp, dc in next dc) 4 times, ch 2, skip next ch-2 sp, join in 3rd ch of beg ch 5. Fasten off after Rnd 20. You will have 7 dc in each dc group. Weave in ends.

PANSY (make 16)

With a double strand of gold, ch 10, join with sl st in first ch to form ring.

Rnd 1: Ch 1, sc in ring, ch 4, sc in ring, ch 6, sc in ring, ch 4, join in first sc.

Rnd 2: Sl st in next ch-4 sp, ch 1, work hdc, dc, 10 tr, and hdc all in same sp, work hdc, dc, 6 tr, 3 dtr, 6 tr, dc and hdc in next ch-6 sp, work hdc, dc, 10 tr, dc and hdc in next ch-4 sp, join in beg ch 1. Fasten off. Weave in ends.

EDGING

Rnd 1: With a double strand of silver, sc in ch-4 sp of any V-st of center, ch 5, *skip next 13 dc, work sc, ch 5 and sc in next dc, ch 5, skip next 3 dc, work sc, ch 5 and sc in next ch-2 sp, (ch 5, skip next ch-2 sp, work sc, ch 5 and sc in next ch-2 sp) 4 times, ch 5, skip next 3 dc, work sc, ch 5 and sc in next dc, ch 5, skip next 3 dc, work sc, ch 5 and sc in ch-4 sp of next point, ch 5; rep from * around, end last rep with sc in ch-4 sp of first point, ch 2, tr in first sc of rnd. This brings thread into position for next rnd.

Rnd 2: Ch 6, *sc in next ch-sp, ch 3, work V-st in next ch-sp, ch 3; rep from * around, end last rep with sc in next ch-sp, ch 3, dc in tr of last rnd, ch 1, dc in 3rd ch of beg ch 6.

Rnd 3: (Ch 3, sc in 3rd ch from hook) 3 times, sc around dc of Rnd 2, ch 4, sc bet 5th and 6th tr of right-hand petal of a pansy, ch 2, skip next 2 ch-sps of center, sc in ch-3 sp of next V-st, ch 4, skip next 2 ch-sps, sc in next V-st, ch 2, sc bet first and 3rd petal of pansy, ch 2, sc in same V-st of center, ch 4, skip next 2 ch-sps of center, sc in next V-st, ch 2, sc bet 5th and 6th tr of left-hand petal of pansy, ch 4, skip next 2 ch-sps, work picot loop in next V-st; rep from * around, end last rep with ch 4, skip 2 ch-sps, join in first sc. Fasten off. Weave in ends.

Floral Scroll Placemats

Size: Approximately 16" by 20".

MATERIALS

DMC Brilliant Knitting/Crochet Cotton—2 balls.
Size 8 steel crochet hook.

Gauge: 3 mesh = 1"; 7 rows = 2".

SPECIAL INSTRUCTIONS

Mesh: Ch 2, skip 2 sts or chs, dc in next st.
Block over block: Dc in each of next 3 sts.
Block over mesh: 2 dc in next ch-2 sp, dc in next dc.
Picot: Ch 4, sc in 3rd ch from hook, ch 1.

Ch 171.
Row 1: Dc in 9th ch from hook, *ch 2, skip 2 chs, dc in next ch; rep from * across—55 mesh.
Row 2: Ch 5, turn on this and every row, skip first dc and ch-2 sp, dc in next dc—1 mesh made; *2 dc in next ch-2 sp; dc in next dc—1 block made; rep from * until you have a total of 53 blocks, ch 2, dc in 3rd ch of beg ch.
Row 3: Ch 5, turn, skip first dc, dc in next dc, work 1 block, 51 mesh, 1 block and 1 mesh.

Beg with Row 4, follow chart until Row 28 is complete, then work Rows 27 through 1 to complete the placemat. Do not fasten off.

EDGING

Ch 1, turn, sl st in first ch of first mesh, ch 1, sc in same mesh; †*ch 3, work picot, ch 3, skip next mesh, sc in next mesh;* rep bet *s to corner, end with sc in corner mesh; work ch 3, picot, ch 3 and sc in corner mesh. Rep from † around, end last rep with join in first sc. Fasten off. Weave in ends.

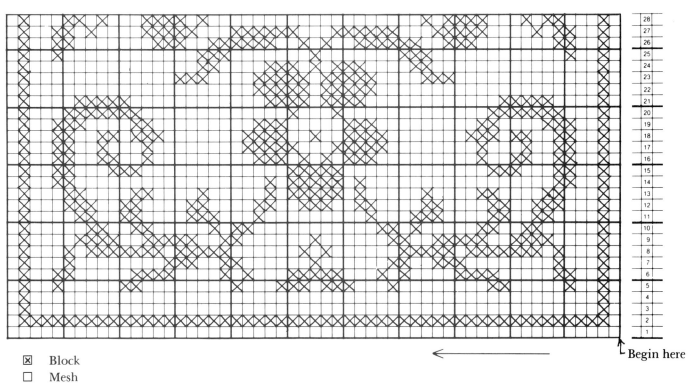

☒   Block
☐   Mesh

←

↳ Begin here

11

Mardi Gras Doily

Size: Approximately 7" in diameter.

MATERIALS

DMC Cordonnet Special, size 30—1 ball white.
DMC Pearl Cotton, size 8—1 ball ombré (any color desired) will make 2 doilies.
Size 10 steel crochet hook.

Gauge: Motif should measure about 1¾" after Rnd 2.

SPECIAL INSTRUCTIONS

Picot: Ch 3, sl st in first ch made.

Ch 8, join with sl st in first ch to form ring.
Rnd 1: Ch 1, 16 sc in ring, join with sl st in first sc.
Rnd 2: Ch 1, sc in same sc and in next sc, *ch 10, turn, sl st in last sc made, turn; keeping thread on wrong side of

work, work 20 sc in ch-10 loop, sl st in same sc of ring, sc in each of next 2 sc; rep from * 7 times, end last rep with sc in next sc, join with sl st in first sc of rnd—8 petals. Fasten off. Weave in ends.

Rnd 3: With right side of work facing, join thread in 10th sc of any petal, ch 4, dc in next sc of same petal, ch 7, *dc in 10th sc of next petal, ch 1, dc in next sc of same petal, ch 7; rep from * around, end last rep with ch 7, join in 3rd ch of beg ch 4.

Rnd 4: Sl st in next ch-1 sp, ch 5, dc in same sp, *ch 3, sc in next ch-7 sp, ch 3, work dc, ch 2, dc in ch-1 sp bet next 2 dc; rep from * around, end last rep with ch 3, join in 3rd ch of beg ch 5,

Rnd 5: Sl st in next ch-2 sp, ch 6, dc in same sp, *ch 3, sc in next ch-3 sp, sc in next sc, sc in next ch-3 sp, ch 3, work dc, ch 3, dc in ch-2 sp bet next 2 dc; rep from * around, end last rep with ch 3, join in 3rd ch of beg ch 6.

Rnd 6: Sl st in ch-3 sp, ch 7, dc in same sp, *ch 3, sc in next ch-3 sp, sc in each of next 3 sc, sc in next ch-3 sp, ch 3, work dc, ch 4, dc in ch-3 sp bet next 2 dc; rep from * around, end last rep with ch 3, join in 3rd ch of beg ch 7.

Rnd 7: Sl st in ch-4 sp, ch 4, 11 tr in same sp, *ch 3, skip next ch-3 sp and sc, sc in each of next 3 sc, ch 3, skip next ch-3 sp, work 12 tr in ch-4 sp bet next 2 dc; rep from * around, end last rep with ch 3, skip next ch-3 sp, join in top of beg ch-4.

Rnd 8: Ch 1, sc in same sp, *work picot, sc in each of next 3 tr, work picot, (sc in same tr as last sc and in each of next 2 tr, work picot) twice, sc in each of next 3 tr, work picot, sc in next tr, ch 4, skip next ch-3 sp and sc, sc in next sc, ch 4, skip next sc and ch-3 sp, sc in first tr of next group; rep from * around, end last rep with ch 4, skip next sc and ch-3 sp, join in first sc.

Rnd 9: Ch 9, *(skip picot and sc following it, dc in next sc, ch 5) 4 times, tr in sc following last picot of group, tr in sc before first picot of next group, ch 5; rep from * around, end last rep with tr in sc following last picot of group, join in 4th ch of beg ch 9.

Rnd 10: Ch 1, *(5 sc in next ch-5 sp) twice, 3 sc in next ch-5 sp, (5 sc in next ch-5 sp) twice; rep from * around, join in first sc.

Rnd 11: Ch 3, *(ch 2, skip next sc, dc in next sc) 11 times, ch 2, dc in next sc; rep from * around, end last rep with ch 2, join in 3rd ch of ch 5.

Rnd 12: Work 2 sc in each ch-sp around; sl st in first sc. Fasten off. Weave in ends.

Rnd 13: Join ombré thread in first sc of last rnd; ch 5, dc in same st, *ch 7, skip next 7 sc, work dc, ch 2 and dc in next sc; rep from * around, end last rep with ch 7, join in 3rd ch of beg ch 5.

Rnd 14: Sl st in next ch-2 sp, ch 5, dc in same sp, *ch 3, sc in next ch-7 sp, ch 3, work dc, ch 2 and dc in ch-2 sp bet next 2 dc; rep from * around, end last rep with ch 3, join in 3rd ch of beg ch 5.

Rnd 15: Sl st in next ch-2 sp, ch 6, dc in same sp, *ch 3, sc in next ch-3 sp, sc in next sc, sc in next ch-3 sp, ch 3, work dc, ch 2 and dc in ch-2 sp bet next 2 dc; rep from * around, end last rep with ch 3, join in 3rd ch of beg ch 6.

Rnd 16: Sl st in next ch-3 sp, ch 7, dc in same sp, *ch 3, sc in next ch-3 sp, sc in each of next 3 sc, sc in next ch-3 sp, ch 3, work dc, ch 4 and dc in ch-3 sp bet next 2 dc; rep from * around, end last rep with ch 3, join in 3rd ch of beg ch 7.

Rnd 17: Sl st in next ch-4 sp, ch 4, 11 tr in same sp, *ch 3, skip next ch-3 sp and sc, sc in each of next 3 sc, skip next ch-3 sp, work 12 tr in ch-4 sp bet next 2 dc; rep from * around, end last rep with ch 3, skip next ch-3 sp, join in top of beg ch-4.

Rnd 18: Ch 1, sc in same sp, *work picot, sc in each of next 3 tr, work picot, (sc in same tr as last sc and in each of next 2 tr, work picot) twice, sc in each of next 3 tr, work picot, sc in next tr, ch 4, skip next ch-3 sp and sc, sc in next sc, ch 4, skip next sc and ch-3 sp, sc in first tr of next group; rep from * around, end last rep with ch 4, skip next sc and ch-3 sp, join in first sc. Fasten off. Weave in ends.

Rose Appliqué Runner

Size: Approximately 36" by 18".

MATERIALS

DMC Brilliant Knitting/Crochet Cotton—3 balls white.
DMC pearl cotton, size 8—1 ball each red ombré and green.
Size 8 steel crochet hook.

Gauge: 3 mesh = 1"; 4 rows = 1".

SPECIAL INSTRUCTIONS

Mesh: Ch 2, skip 2 sts or chs, dc in next st.
Block over block: Dc in each of next 3 sts.
Block over mesh: 2 dc in ch-2 sp, dc in next dc.
Dec at beg of row: Ch 1, turn, sl st in each of first 22 sts, ch 3, complete row.
Dec at end of row: Do not work over last 8 blocks.
Spiderweb—Row 1: Work 6 blocks.
Row 2: Work 2 mesh, ch 11, skip 5 dc, dc in next dc, work 2 mesh.
Row 3: Work 1 mesh, ch 6, skip next mesh, sc in 6th ch of ch 11, ch 6, skip next dc and ch-sp, dc in next dc, work 1 mesh.

Row 4: Ch 8, skip 1 mesh, sc in next ch-6 sp, sc in next sc, sc in next ch-6 sp, ch 8, skip next dc and ch-sp, dc in next dc.
Row 5: Ch 8, skip ch-6 sp, sc in each of next 3 sc, ch 8, skip ch-6 sp, dc in next dc.
Row 6: Ch 2, skip 2 chs of ch 8, dc in next ch, ch 8, skip ch-sp and next sc, sc in next sc, ch 8, skip next sc and 5 chs of ch 8, dc in next ch, ch 2, skip next 2 chs, dc in next dc.
Row 7: Work 1 mesh, ch 2, skip 2 chs of ch 8, dc in next ch, ch 5, skip next ch-sp, sc and 5 chs of next ch 8, dc in next ch, ch 2, skip 2 chs, dc in next dc.

The runner is made up of 3 identical sections, each worked from the center out.

Ch 112.
Row 1: Dc in 4th ch from hook and in each of next 24 chs—8 blocks; work 20 mesh and 8 blocks.
Row 2: Ch 2, turn, work 1 block, work Row 2 of spiderweb over next 6 blocks, work 1 block, 20 mesh and 1 block, work Row 2 of spiderweb over next 6 blocks, work 1 block.

14

Row 3: Ch 2, turn, work 1 block, Row 3 of spiderweb, 1 block, 20 mesh, 1 block, Row 3 of spiderweb and 1 block.
Row 4: Ch 3, turn, work 1 block, spiderweb, 1 block, 20 mesh, 1 block, spiderweb and 1 block.
Rows 5 and 6: Ch 2, turn, work 1 block, spiderweb, 1 block, 20 mesh, 1 block, spiderweb and 1 block.
Row 7: Ch 3, turn, work 1 block, spiderweb, 1 block, 20 mesh, 1 block, spiderweb and 1 block.
Row 8: Ch 2, turn, work 3 blocks, 5 dc in ch-5 sp of spiderweb, work 10 blocks, 6 mesh, 10 blocks, 5 dc in ch-5 sp of spiderweb, work 3 blocks.

Beg with Row 9, follow chart through Row 36. Ch 3 to beg every 3rd row, ch 2 to beg all other rows. Fasten off after Row 36. Turn section so that Row 1 is at top. Join thread in first st, ch 2 and work as for first half. Weave in ends. Make 2 more sections the same.

The sections are joined along the side edges. Attach the thread to the top of Row 22 on one section, ch 3, sc in the corresponding place on the next section, *ch 3, sc around the end stitch of the next row on the first section, ch 3, sc around the end stitch of the following row on the second section; rep from *, working in every other row of each section. Join the remaining section in the same way.

ROSE (make 3).

With red, ch 8, join with sl st in first ch to form ring.
Rnd 1: Ch 5, *dc in ring, ch 2; rep from * 6 times, join with sl st in 3rd ch of beg ch 5.
Rnd 2: Work sc, 4 dc and sc in each ch-sp, join in first sc.
Rnd 3: Ch 2; working from the back, insert the hook around the ch 3 at the beg of Rnd 1 and work 1 sc; ch 4, *sc around next dc of Rnd 1, ch 4; rep from * around, join in first sc.
Rnd 4: Holding petals forward, work sc, 6 dc and sc in each ch-sp, join in first sc.
Rnd 5: Ch 2; from back, sc around first sc of Rnd 3; ch 5, *sc around next sc of Rnd 3, ch 5; rep from * around, join in first sc.
Rnd 6: Holding petals forward, work sc, 2 dc, 2 tr, 2 dc and sc in each ch-sp, join in first sc.
Rnd 7: *Ch 6, sc bet last sc of this petal and first sc of next petal; rep from * around, end with sl st in base of first ch 6.
Rnd 8: Work 10 sc in each ch-sp, join in first sc.
Rnd 9: Sl st in each of next 6 sts, *ch 6, skip 6 sc, sl st in each of next 4 sc; rep from * around, end with ch 6, skip next 3 sc and 3 sl sts, sl st in next sl st. Fasten off.
Rnd 10: Ch 3, *work 12 dc in next ch-6 sp; rep from * 6 times, work 11 dc in next ch-6 sp, join in top of beg ch 3. Fasten off. Weave in ends.

LEAF (make 18)

With green, ch 11, sc in 2nd ch from hook and in each rem ch.
Rnd 1: Ch 1, turn, *sc in next st, hdc in next st, dc in each of next 2 sts, tr in each of next 2 sts, dc in each of next 2 sts, hdc in next st, sc in next st,* ch 3, working on opposite side of starting ch, rep bet *s.
Rnd 2: Ch 1, turn, sc in each of next 10 sts, 3 sc in ch-3 sp, sc in each of next 10 sts. Fasten off. Weave in ends.

Sew a rose and 6 leaves to the center of each section of the runner.

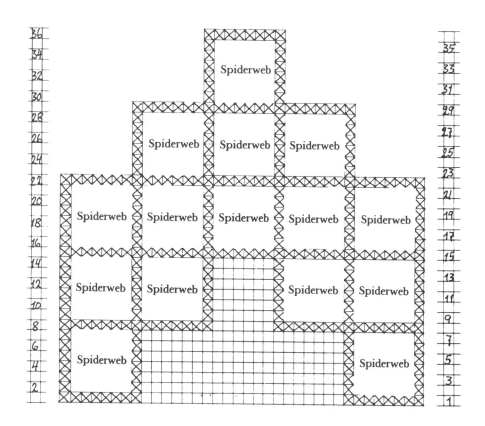

| ☒ | Block |
| ☐ | Mesh |

Peacock Feather
Centerpiece

Size: Approximately 24" in diameter.

MATERIALS

DMC Brilliant Knitting/Crochet Cotton—2 balls.
Size 6 steel crochet hook.

Gauge: Piece should measure approximately 3½" in diameter after Rnd 4.

SPECIAL INSTRUCTIONS

Picot: Ch 5, sl st in 4th ch from hook, ch 1.

Cluster: Holding back last lp of each st on hook, work specified number of sts, yo and draw through all lps on hook.

Ch 8, join with sl st in first ch to form ring.
Rnd 1: Ch 3, work 23 dc in ring, join with sl st in top of beg ch 3.
Rnd 2: Ch 5, *tr in next dc, ch 1; rep from * around, sl st in 4th ch of beg ch 5 and in first ch-1 sp.
Rnd 3: Ch 6, *tr in next ch-1 sp, ch 2; rep from * around, sl st in 4th ch of beg ch 6 and in first ch-2 sp.

Rnd 4: Ch 4, 2 tr in same sp, tr in next tr, 3 tr in next ch-2 sp, *ch 2, 3 tr in next sp, tr in next tr, 3 tr in next sp; rep from * 10 times, dc in top of beg ch 4 to bring thread into position for the next rnd—12 groups of 7 tr each.

Rnd 5: Ch 4, 2 tr around dc just made, ch 2, 3 tr in same sp, *ch 2, work 3 tr, ch 2, 3 tr in next ch-2 sp; rep from * around, end last rep with ch 2, sl st in top of beg ch 4, next 2 tr and next ch-2 sp.

Rnd 6: Ch 4, 2 tr in same sp, ch 2, 3 tr in same sp; *ch 4, skip next ch-2 sp, work 3 tr, ch 2, 3 tr in next sp; rep from * around, end last rep with ch 4, sl st in top of beg ch 4, 2 tr and first ch-2 sp.

Rnd 7: Ch 4, 2 tr in same sp, ch 2, 3 tr in same sp; *ch 6, skip next ch-4 sp, work 3 tr, ch 2, 3 tr in next ch-2 sp; rep from * around, end last rep with ch 6, sl st in top of beg ch 4, 2 tr and first ch-2 sp.

Rnd 8: Ch 4, 8 tr in same sp, *ch 8, skip next ch-6 sp, 9 tr in next ch-2 sp; rep from * around, end last rep with ch 8, join in top of beg ch 4.

Rnd 9: Ch 4, tr in same sp, *(tr in next tr, ch 1, skip next tr) 3 times, tr in next tr, 2 tr in next tr, ch 8, skip next ch-8 sp, 2 tr in first tr of next group; rep from * around, end last rep with ch 8, join in top of beg ch 4.

Rnd 10: Ch 4, tr in same sp, *tr in next tr, ch 1, work 3-tr cluster in next ch-sp, ch 1, tr in next ch-1 sp, ch 1, 3-tr cluster in next ch-sp, ch 1, skip next tr, tr in next tr, 2 tr in last tr of group, ch 7, 2 tr in first tr of next group; rep from * around, end last rep with ch 7, join in top of beg ch 4.

Rnd 11: Ch 4, tr in same sp, *tr in next tr, ch 1, skip next tr, 3-tr cluster in next sp, ch 1, skip cluster, tr in next sp, tr in next tr, tr in next sp, ch 1, skip cluster, 3-tr cluster in next sp, ch 1, skip next tr, tr in next tr, 2 tr in last tr of group, ch 6, 2 tr in first tr of next group; rep from * around, end last rep with ch 6, join in top of ch 4.

Rnd 12: Ch 4, tr in same sp, *tr in next st, ch 1, skip next tr, 3-tr cluster in next sp, ch 1, skip cluster, tr in next sp, tr in each of next 3 tr, tr in next sp, ch 1, skip cluster, 3-tr cluster in next ch-sp, ch 1, skip next tr, tr in next tr, 2 tr in last tr of group, ch 6, 2 tr in first tr of next group; rep from * around, end last rep with ch 6, join in top of beg ch 4.

Rnd 13: Ch 4, tr in same sp, *tr in next tr, skip next tr, ch 2, 3-tr cluster in next ch-sp, ch 1, skip cluster, tr in next sp, tr in each of next 5 tr, tr in next ch-sp, ch 1, skip cluster, 3-tr cluster in next ch-sp, ch 2, skip next tr, tr in next tr, 2 tr in last tr of group, ch 5, 2 tr in first tr of next group; rep from * around, end last rep with ch 5, join in top of beg ch 4.

Rnd 14: Ch 4, tr in same sp, *tr in next st, ch 2, skip next tr, 3-tr cluster in next ch-sp, ch 1, skip cluster, tr in next sp, tr in each of next 7 tr, tr in next ch-sp, ch 1, skip cluster, 3-tr cluster in next ch-sp, ch 2, skip next tr, tr in next tr, 2 tr in last tr of group, ch 5, 2 tr in first tr of next group; rep from * around, end last rep with ch 5, join in top of beg ch 4.

Rnd 15: Ch 4, tr in each of next 2 tr, *ch 2, skip next sp and cluster, 3-tr cluster in next sp, ch 1, tr in each of next 9 tr, ch 1, 3-tr cluster in next sp, ch 2, skip cluster and next sp, tr in each of last 3 tr of group, ch 7, tr in each of first 3 tr of next group; rep from * around, end last rep with ch 7, join in top of beg ch 4.

Rnd 16: Ch 4, tr in each of next 2 tr, *ch 2, skip next sp and cluster, 3-tr cluster in next sp, ch 1, skip next tr, tr in

each of next 7 tr, ch 1, skip next tr, 3-tr cluster in next sp, ch 2, skip cluster and next sp, tr in each of last 3 tr of group, ch 11, tr in each of first 3 tr of next group; rep from * around, end last rep with ch 11, join in top of beg ch 4.

Rnd 17: Ch 4, tr in each of next 2 tr, *ch 2, skip next sp and cluster, 3-tr cluster in next sp, ch 1, skip next tr, tr in each of next 5 tr, ch 1, skip next tr, 3-tr cluster in next sp, ch 2, skip cluster and next sp, tr in each of last 3 tr of group, ch 16, tr in each of first 3 tr of next group; rep from * around, end last rep with ch 16, join in top of beg ch 4.

Rnd 18: Ch 4, tr in each of next 2 tr, *ch 2, skip next sp and cluster, 3-tr cluster in next sp, ch 1, skip next tr, tr in each of next 3 tr, ch 1, skip next tr, 3-tr cluster in next sp, ch 2, skip cluster and next sp, tr in each of last 3 tr of group, ch 8, dtr in ch-16 sp, ch 1, dtr in same sp, ch 8, tr in each of first 3 tr of next group; rep from * around, end last rep with dtr in ch-16 sp, ch 1, dtr in same sp, ch 8, join in top of beg ch 4.

Rnd 19: Ch 4, tr in each of next 2 tr, *ch 2, skip next sp and cluster, 3-tr cluster in next sp, ch 1, skip next tr, tr in next tr, skip next tr, 3-tr cluster in next sp, ch 2, skip cluster and next sp, tr in each of last 3 tr of group, ch 12, skip ch-8 sp and next dtr, work dtr, ch 1, dtr in ch-1 sp, ch 12, skip next tr and ch-8 sp, tr in each of first 3 tr of next group; rep from * around, end last rep with ch 12, join in top of beg ch 4.

Rnd 20: Ch 4, tr in each of next 2 tr, *ch 2, skip next sp and cluster, 3-tr cluster in next sp, ch 1, skip next tr, 3-tr cluster in next sp, ch 2, skip cluster and next sp, tr in each of last 3 tr of group, ch 14, skip ch-12 sp and next dtr, work dtr, ch 3, dtr in ch-1 sp, ch 14, skip next dtr and ch-12 sp, tr in each of first 3 tr of next group; rep from * around, end last rep with ch 14, join in top of beg ch 4.

Rnd 21: Ch 4, tr in each of next 2 tr, *ch 2, skip next sp and cluster, 3-tr cluster in next sp, ch 2, skip cluster and next sp, tr in each of last 3 tr of group, ch 15, skip ch-14 sp, dtr in next dtr, 5 dtr in ch-3 sp, dtr in next dtr, ch 15, skip ch-14 sp, tr in each of first 3 tr of next group; rep from * around, end last rep with ch 15, join in top of beg ch 4.

Rnd 22: Ch 4, tr in each of next 2 tr, *ch 1, skip next sp, cluster and sp, tr in each of next 3 tr, ch 15, skip ch-15 sp, 3-*dtr* cluster in first dtr, ch 15, skip next 5 tr, 3-dtr cluster in next dtr, ch 15, skip ch-15 sp, tr in each of first 3 tr of next group; rep from * around, end last rep with ch 15, join in top of beg ch 4.

Rnd 23: Ch 4, tr in each of next 2 tr, *tr in next sp, tr in each of next 3 tr, ch 13, skip ch-15 sp and cluster, 25 dtr in next sp, ch 13, skip cluster and ch-15 sp, tr in each of next 3 tr; rep from * around, end last rep with ch 13, join in top of beg ch 4.

Rnd 24: Sl st in next st, ch 4, tr in each of next 4 tr, ch 9, skip ch-13 sp, *(dtr in next dtr, ch 1, skip next dtr) 12 times, dtr in next dtr, ch 9, skip ch-13 sp and next tr, tr in each of next 5 tr; rep from * around, end last rep with ch 9, join in top of beg ch 4.

Rnd 25: Sl st in next st, ch 3, work 2-*tr* cluster over next 2 tr, ch 9, skip next tr, ch-9 sp and first dtr, *(4-tr cluster in next ch-sp, work picot) 12 times, ch 9, skip next tr, ch-9 sp and next tr, 3-tr cluster over next 3 tr; rep from * around, end last rep with ch 9, join in top of beg ch 3. Fasten off. Weave in ends.

Ribbon-Crochet Runner

Size: Approximately 51" by 17".

MATERIALS

DMC Brilliant Knitting/Crochet Cotton—3 balls.
Size 8 steel crochet hook.

Gauge: 9 rows = 2".

SPECIAL INSTRUCTIONS

Basic ribbon: Ch 10, dc in 7th ch from hook and each of rem 3 chs. *Ch 6, turn; dc in each of 4 dc. Rep from * to desired length.
Join to a lp: Sc in the specified lp.
Join to a lp with dc: Dc in the specified lp.
Join 3 lps: At the beg of the row, ch 3, insert the hook through the last 2 lps on the same side and draw up a lp. Yo and draw through 2 lps to complete an sc. Ch 3, turn, dc in each of the 4 dc of the ribbon. Join 4 lps and 5 lps in the same way.

Cluster: *Yo twice and draw up a lp in sp, (yo and draw through 2 lps) twice; rep from * twice—4 lps on hook; yo and draw through all 4 lps.

The runner is made up of 3 motifs. For each motif, work the basic ribbon, joining the ch-lps on the edge as specified in the instructions.

FIRST SECTION OF MOTIF

Beg at A on chart and work basic ribbon until 8 lps have been completed.
9th lp: Join to 7th, 5th and 3rd lps—4 lps joined.
  Continue to work ribbon, joining as follows.
18th lp: Join to 16th, 14th, 12th and 10th lps—5 lps joined.
20th lp: Join to 8th lp (next free lp).
25th lp: Join 4 lps.
34th lp: Join 5 lps.
36th lp: Join to 24th lp (next free lp).

41st lp: Join 4 lps.
50th lp: Join 5 lps.
57th lp: Join 4 lps.
66th lp: Join 5 lps.
68th lp: Join to 56th lp (next free lp).
70th lp: Join 5 lps with dtr as follows—ch 7, dtr in each of next 4 free lps, ch 1, turn; sl st in each dtr and in each of next 5 chs, ch 3, dc in each of 4 dc of ribbon.
72nd lp: Join to 4th lp.
73rd lp: Join 4 lps.
74th lp: Join to 2nd lp.
85th lp: Join 4 lps.
93rd lp: Join 4 lps.
97th lp: Join to 77th lp with dc.
99th lp: Join to 65th lp.
101st lp: Join to 63rd lp.
102nd lp: Join 5 lps.
104th lp: Join to 92nd lp.
109th lp: Join 4 lps.
118th lp: Join 5 lps.
120th lp: Join to 108th lp.
125th lp: Join 4 lps.
134th lp: Join 5 lps.
136th lp: Join to 124th lp.
138th lp: Join 4 lps with dc as follows—ch 5, dc in each of next 3 free lps, ch 1, turn; sl st in each dc and in each of next 3 chs, ch 3, dc in each of 4 dc of ribbon.

140th lp: Join to 88th lp.
141st lp: Join 4 lps.
149th lp: Join 4 lps.
151st lp: Join to 133rd lp with dc.
  Work 1 more loop and place a marker.

SECOND SECTION

Work as for first section with the following additions.
First lp: Join to 131st lp of last section.
11th lp: Join to 129th lp of last section.
13th lp: Join to 127th lp of last section.
76th lp: Join to 152nd lp of last section.
78th lp: Join to 150th lp of last section.
80th lp: Join to 148th lp of last section.

THIRD SECTION

Work as for second section.

FOURTH SECTION

Work as for second section, joining it to the 3rd section as before. Mark the 46th lp to be joined to the center. Being very careful not to twist the crochet, join to the first section as follows.
127th lp: Join to 13th lp.
129th lp: Join to 11th lp.
131st lp: Join to the first lp.

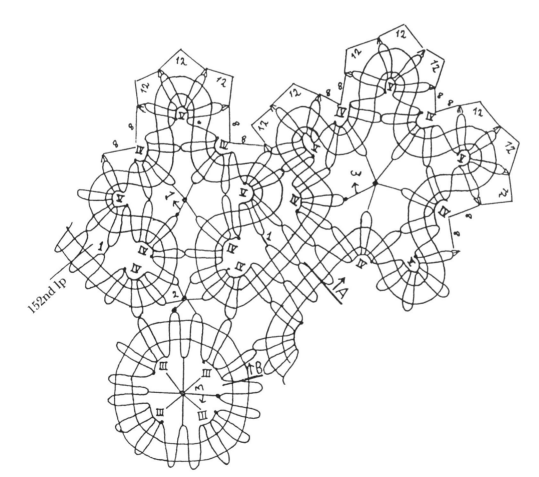

III—Join 3 lps
IV—Join 4 lps
 V—Join 5 lps
 1—Join lps with dc
 2—Join lps with tr
 3—Join lps with dtr
 8—Chain 8
12—Chain 12
⋀ —Cluster

19

148th lp: Join to 80th lp.
150th lp: Join to 78th lp.
152nd lp: Join to 76th lp. Fasten off and sew the last row of the ribbon to the first row of the ribbon. Weave in the ends. Remove the markers placed in the last lp of each section.

CENTER

Beg ribbon and work 1 lp.
2nd lp: Join to marked lp of motif.
4th lp: Join to next free lp of motif.
5th lp: Join 3 lps.
8th lp: Ch 6, tr in first free lp of center, tr in each of next 4 free lps on motif, ch 1, turn; sl st in each of last 5 tr and in each of next 4 chs, ch 3, dc in each of 4 dc of ribbon.
10th lp: Join to next free lp of motif.
12th lp: Join to next free lp of motif.
13th lp: Join 3 lps.
16th lp: Rep 8th lp.
18th lp: Join to next free lp of motif.
20th lp: Join to next free lp of motif.
21st lp: Join 3 lps.
24th lp: Rep 8th lp.
26th lp: Join to next free lp of motif.

28th lp: Join to next free lp of motif.
29th lp: Join 3 lps.
31st lp: Join 4 lps with dtr.
32nd lp: Rep 8th lp. Fasten off. Sew last row to first row. Weave in ends.

EDGING

Attach thread in 17th lp of any section of motif (C on chart), ch 4, *yo twice and draw up a lp in sp, (yo and draw through 2 lps) twice*; rep bet *s twice—3 lps on hook, yo and draw through all 3 lps on hook. **Ch 8, sc in next joining, ch 8, cluster in next lp, (ch 12, cluster in next lp) 3 times, ch 8, sc in next joining, ch 8, cluster in next lp, (ch 12, cluster in next free lp) 3 times, ch 8, sc in next joining, ch 8, (cluster in next lp, ch 12) twice, cluster in next joining, ch 8, sc in next joining, ch 8, cluster in next lp, (ch 12, cluster in next lp) 3 times, ch 8, sc in next joining, ch 8, cluster in next joining, (ch 12, cluster in next lp) twice. Rep from ** around, end last rep with cluster in last joining, ch 12, cluster in next lp, ch 12, join in top of first cluster. Fasten off. Weave in ends.

Make 2 more motifs and sew them together as in photograph. Starch runner heavily and block carefully.

Hexagonal Centerpiece

Size: Approximately 35″ point to point.
Each edge measures about 30″

MATERIALS

DMC Cordonnet Special, size 30—8 balls.
Size 12 steel crochet hook.

Gauge: Each motif is about 4¼″ in diameter.

FIRST MOTIF

Ch 11, join with sl st in first ch to form ring.
Rnd 1: Ch 2, work 23 hdc in ring, join with sl st in top of beg ch 2.
Rnd 2: Ch 4, *dc in back lp of next st, ch 1; rep from * around, join in 3rd ch of beg ch 4, sl st in next ch-sp.
Rnd 3: Ch 7, *skip next ch-1 sp, dc in next ch-1 sp, ch 4; rep from * around, join in 3rd ch of beg ch 7, sl st in next ch-sp—12 sps.
Rnd 4: Ch 4, work tr, ch 3, 2 tr in same sp, ch 5, *work 2 tr, ch 3, 2 tr in next ch-4 sp, ch 5; rep from * around, join in top of beg ch 4, sl st in next tr and ch-sp.
Rnd 5: Ch 4, work tr, ch 3, 2 tr in same sp, *ch 3, skip next 2 tr, sc in next ch-5 sp, ch 3, skip next 2 tr, work 2 tr, ch 3, 2 tr in next ch-3 sp; rep from * around, end last rep after sc with ch 3, join in top of beg ch 4, sl st in next tr and ch-sp.
Rnd 6: Ch 4, work tr, ch 3, 2 tr in same sp, *ch 3, skip next 2 tr, sc in next ch-3 sp, ch 2, skip next sc, sc in next ch-3 sp,

ch 3, skip next 2 tr, work 2 tr, ch 3, 2 tr in next ch-3 sp; rep from * around, end last rep with join in top of beg ch 4. Fasten off. Weave in ends. This motif will be at the center of the cloth.

SECOND MOTIF

Work as for first motif through Rnd 5.
Rnd 6: Ch 4, work tr, ch 3, 2 tr in same sp, *ch 3, skip next 2 tr, sc in next ch-3 sp, ch 2, skip next sc, sc in next ch-3 sp, ch 3, skip next 2 tr, work 2 tr, ch 3, 2 tr in next ch-3 sp; rep from * 8 times, **ch 3, skip next 2 tr, sc in next ch-3 sp, ch 2, skip next sc, sc in next ch-3 sp, skip next 2 tr, 2 tr in next ch-3 sp, ch 1, sc in corresponding sp of first motif, ch 1, 2 tr in same sp of second motif;** rep between **s once more, complete rnd as for first motif.

Join the third motif to the two points to the right of the joining on the first motif and the two points to the left of the joining on the second motif. Make and join 4 more motifs to form a ring around the center motif. The seventh motif will be joined to the first, 7th and 2nd motifs.

Continue to make and join 5 more rnds of motifs around the center. Each rnd will have 6 more motifs than the previous rnd. The last rnd will have 36 motifs.

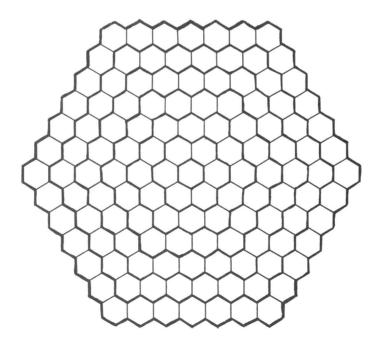

Spring Garland Tablecloth

Size: Approximately 32" in diameter.

MATERIALS

DMC Brilliant Knitting/Crochet Cotton—2 balls white, 1 ball green, 2 balls yellow ombré.
Size 6 steel crochet hook.

Gauge: Center should measure about 4½" in diameter after Rnd 5.

SPECIAL INSTRUCTIONS

Picot: Ch 5, sc in 5th ch from hook.
Cluster: *Yo twice, draw up a lp in sp indicated, (yo and draw through 2 lps) twice. Rep from * once for 2-tr cluster, twice for 3-tr cluster or 3 times for 4-tr cluster. Yo and draw through all lps on hook.

CENTER

With white, ch 10, join with sl st in first ch to form ring.
Rnd 1: Ch 4, work 23 tr in ring, join with sl st in top of beg ch 4.
Rnd 2: Ch 5, *tr in next tr, ch 1; rep from * around, join with sl st in 4th ch of beg ch 5—24 ch-sps.
Rnd 3: Sl st in first ch-1 sp, ch 4, 2 tr in same sp, *3 tr in next ch-1 sp; rep from * around, join with sl st in top of first ch 4—72 sts.
Rnd 4: Ch 6, *skip next tr, tr in next tr, ch 2; rep from * around, join with sl st in 4th ch of beg ch 6—36 ch-sps.
Rnd 5: Rep Rnd 3—108 sts.
Rnd 6: Ch 4, tr in each of next 5 tr, *ch 6, skip next 3 tr, tr in each of next 6 tr; rep from * around, end with ch 6, join in top of beg ch 4—12 tr groups.

Rnd 7: Ch 4, tr in each of next 5 tr, *ch 8, tr in each of next 6 tr; rep from * around, end with ch 8, join in top of beg ch 4.

Rnd 8: Ch 4, tr in each of next 5 tr, *ch 10, tr in each of next 6 tr; rep from * around, end with ch 10, join in top of beg ch 4.

Rnd 9: Ch 4, tr in each of next 5 tr, *ch 12, tr in each of next 6 tr; rep from * around, end with ch 12, join in top of beg ch 4.

Rnd 10: Ch 4, tr in same sp as sl st, tr in each of next 2 tr, *ch 2, tr in each of next 2 tr, 2 tr in last tr of group, ch 10, 2 tr in first st of next tr group, tr in each of next 2 tr; rep from * around, end last rep with ch 10, join in top of beg ch 4.

Rnd 11: Ch 4, tr in same sp as sl st, tr in each of next 2 tr, 2 tr in next tr, *ch 2, skip next ch-2 sp, 2 tr in next tr, tr in each of next 2 tr, 2 tr in last tr of group, ch 8, 2 tr in first tr of next group, tr in each of next 2 tr, 2 tr in next tr; rep from * around, end last rep with ch 8, join in top of beg ch 4.

Rnd 12: Ch 4, tr in same sp as sl st, tr in each of next 4 tr, 2 tr in next tr, *ch 2, skip next ch-2 sp, 2 tr in next tr, tr in each of next 4 tr, 2 tr in last tr of group, ch 6, 2 tr in first tr of next group, tr in each of next 4 tr, 2 tr in next tr; rep from * around, end last rep with ch 6, join in top of beg ch 4.

Rnd 13: Ch 4, tr in same sp as sl st, tr in each of next 7 tr, *ch 4, skip next ch-2 sp, tr in each of next 7 tr, 2 tr in last tr of group, ch 4, 2 tr in first tr of next group, tr in each of next 7 tr; rep from * around, end last rep with ch 4, join in top of beg ch 4.

Rnd 14: Ch 4, tr in same sp as sl st, tr in each of next 6 tr, work 2-tr cluster over next 2 tr, *ch 8, skip next ch-4 sp, work 2-tr cluster over next 2 tr, tr in each of next 6 tr, 2 tr in last tr of group, ch 3, 2 tr in first tr of next group, tr in each of next 6 tr, work 2-tr cluster over next 2 tr; rep from * around, end last rep with ch 3, join in top of beg ch 4.

Rnd 15: Ch 4, tr in same sp as sl st, tr in each of next 6 tr, work 2-tr cluster over next 2 tr, *ch 4, work tr, ch 4, tr all in ch-8 sp, ch 4, work 2-tr cluster over next 2 tr, tr in each of next 6 tr, 2 tr in last tr of group, ch 2, 2 tr in first tr of next group, tr in each of next 6 tr, work 2-tr cluster over next 2 tr; rep from * around, end last rep with ch 2, join in top of beg ch 4.

Rnd 16: Ch 4, work 2-tr cluster over next 2 tr, tr in each of next 4 tr, work 2-tr cluster over next 2 tr, *(ch 4, tr in next ch-sp) 3 times, ch 4, work 2-tr cluster over next 2 tr, tr in each of next 5 tr, work 2-tr cluster over last 2 tr of group, ch 4, work 2-tr cluster over first 2 tr of next group, tr in each of next 5 tr, work 2-tr cluster over next 2 tr; rep from * around, end last rep with ch 4, join in top of beg ch 4.

Rnd 17: Ch 4, work 2-tr cluster over next 2 tr, tr in each of next 2 tr, work 2-tr cluster over next 2 tr, *(ch 4, tr in next ch-sp) 4 times, ch 4, work 2-tr cluster over next 2 tr, tr in each of next 3 tr, work 2-tr cluster over last 2 tr of group, ch 6, work 2-tr cluster over first 2 tr of next group, tr in each of next 3 tr, work 2-tr cluster over next 2 tr; rep from * around, end last rep with ch 6, join in top of first cluster.

Rnd 18: Ch 3, work 3-tr cluster over next 3 tr, *(ch 4, tr in next ch-sp) 5 times, ch 4, skip next tr, work 4-tr cluster over next 4 tr, ch 4, tr in ch-6 sp, ch 4, skip next st, work 4-tr cluster over next 4 tr; rep from * around, end last rep with join in top of first cluster.

Rnd 19: Ch 8, work 2-tr cluster over st just worked in and next tr, *ch 4, work 2-tr cluster over last tr worked in and next tr; rep from * around, end with ch 4, tr in last tr worked in, sl st in 4th ch of beg ch 8—96 ch-sps. Fasten off. Weave in ends.

Rnd 20: With white, ch 12, dc in 8th ch from hook and in each rem ch, ch 3. From right side of cloth, work 3-tr cluster in any ch-4 sp of Rnd 19, ch 3. Turn work; *dc in each of first 2 dc, ch 1, skip next dc, dc in each of last 2 dc. Turn work; ch 7, dc in each of first 2 dc, dc in ch-1 sp, dc in each of last 2 dc, ch 3, work 3-tr cluster in next ch-4 sp of Rnd 19, ch 3. Turn work. Rep from * around until you have 96 clusters. After last cluster, ch 3, turn work, dc in each of first 2 dc, ch 1, skip next dc, dc in each of last 2 dc. Fasten off, leaving an end for sewing. Sew first 5 sts of rnd to last 5 sts. Weave in ends.

Rnd 21: Join white with sl st in any ch-7 lp of Rnd 20. Ch 3, work 2-tr cluster in same lp, *ch 7, work 3-tr cluster in next ch-7 lp; rep from * around, end with ch 7, join in top of first cluster. Fasten off. Weave in ends.

Rnd 22: With green, sc in any ch-7 sp, work picot, sc in same sp, *ch 6, work sc, picot, sc in next ch-7 sp; rep from * around, end with sc, picot and sc in last sp, ch 2, dtr in first sc of rnd to bring thread into position for next rnd.

Rnd 23: Work sc, picot and sc around dtr just made, *ch 8, work sc, picot and sc in next ch-6 sp; rep from * around, end with sc, picot and sc in last sp, ch 3, tr tr in first sc of rnd. Do not fasten off. Remove hook and put center aside.

FIRST FLOWER

With yellow, ch 6, join with sl st in first ch to form ring.
Rnd 1: Ch 6, *tr in ring, ch 2; rep from * 6 times, join in 4th ch of beg ch 6.
Rnd 2: Sl st in first ch-2 sp, ch 4, 3 tr in same sp, *ch 2, 4 tr in next ch-2 sp; rep from * around, join in top of beg ch 4.
Rnd 3: Ch 4, tr in same sp, tr in each of next 2 tr, 2 tr in next tr, *ch 3, 2 tr in next tr, tr in each of next 2 tr, 2 tr in next tr; rep from * around, end with ch 3, join in top of first ch 4.
Rnd 4: Sl st in first tr, ch 4, work a 3-tr cluster over next 3 tr, *ch 10, sc in ch-3 sp, ch 10, skip next tr, work a 4-tr cluster over next 4 tr; rep from * around, end last rep with ch 10, join in top of first cluster. Fasten off.

SECOND FLOWER

Work as for first flower through Rnd 3.
Rnd 4: Sl st in first tr, ch 4, work a 3-tr cluster over next 3 tr, (ch 10, sc in next ch-3 sp, ch 10, skip next tr, work a 4-tr cluster over next 4 tr) twice, *ch 4, sc in corresponding ch-10 lp of first flower, ch 4,* sc in next ch-3 sp of second flower, rep bet *s once, complete rnd as for first flower.

Make and join a total of 24 flowers to form a ring, leaving 4 ch-10 lps free on the inner edge of the ring and 8 ch-lps free on the outer edge. The 24th flower will be joined to both the 23rd flower and the first flower.

FINISHING

Joining Rnd: Pick up center and insert hook in dropped lp, work sc, picot and sc around the tr tr made at the end of the last rnd of the center, ch 4, tr in first free ch-lp on inner edge of any flower, *ch 4, work sc, picot and sc in next ch-8 sp of center, (ch 4, sc in next ch-lp of flower, ch 4, work sc, picot and sc in next ch-8 sp of center) twice, ch 4, tr in last free ch-lp of flower, ch 4, work sc, picot and sc in next ch-8 sp of center, ch 4, tr in first free ch-lp on next flower. Rep from * around, end last rep with ch 4, join in first sc. Fasten off.

Next Rnd: With green, sc in 2nd free ch-lp on outer edge of any flower, work picot and sc in same ch-lp, *(ch 8, work sc, picot and sc in next ch-lp) 5 times, ch 8, pick up a lp in next ch-lp of same flower, pick up a lp in first ch-lp of next flower, yo and draw through all 3 lps on hook, ch 8, work sc, picot and sc in next ch-lp; rep from * around, end after last picot group with ch 3, tr tr in first sc.

Last Rnd: Work sc, picot and sc around tr tr just made, *(ch 4, work picot, ch 4, work sc, picot and sc in next ch-sp) 6 times, ch 4, work sc, picot and sc in first ch-sp of next flower; rep from * around, ending after last ch 4 with sl st in first sc. Fasten off. Weave in all ends.

Floral Fantasy Doily

Size: Approximately 13½″ in diameter.

MATERIALS

DMC Cordonnet Special, size 20—1 ball white, 1 ball red.
DMC Pearl Cotton, size 8—1 ball green ombré #92.
DMC gold embroidery thread, size 10—1 spool.
Size 10 steel crochet hook.

Gauge: Each flower measures about 2¼″ across.

SPECIAL INSTRUCTIONS

Shell: 3 dc, ch 3, 3 dc all in same sp.

For this centerpiece, the flowers are worked first, then the edging and finally the center.

FLOWER (make 8)

With red, ch 10, join with sl st in first ch to form ring.
Rnd 1: Work 16 sc in ring, join with sl st in first sc.
Rnd 2: Ch 6, dc in same st as sl st, *skip next sc, work dc, ch 3, dc in next dc; rep from * 6 times, skip next sc, join in 3rd ch of beg ch 6, sl st in next ch-3 sp—8 dc groups.
Rnd 3: Ch 3, work dc, ch 3 and 2 dc in same sp, *work 2 dc, ch 3, 2 dc in next ch-3 sp; rep from * around, join in top of beg ch 3, sl st in next dc and ch-3 sp.
Rnd 4: Ch 3, work 2 dc, ch 3, 3 dc in same sp—first shell completed, *work shell in next ch-3 sp; rep from * around, join in top of beg ch-3 sp, sl st in each of next 2 dc and in next ch-3 sp.
Rnd 5: Ch 3, 9 dc in same sp, *10 dc in next ch-3 sp; rep from * around, join in top of beg ch-3. Fasten off. Weave in ends.
Gold trim: Draw up a double strand of gold thread in sc bet any 2 dc groups of Rnd 1. *Work 5 sl sts (1 on each rnd) bet dc-groups out to edge of flower. Sl st in back lp of each dc of next dc group, sl st bet groups in each rnd to center. Rep from * around, end at center. Fasten off. Weave in ends.

Edging: With green, ch 5, join with sl st in first ch to form ring. Ch 3, work 2 dc, ch 3, 3 dc in ring—first shell completed. Ch 3, sc in 3rd dc of a dc group of any flower. Ch 3, turn, shell in ch-3 sp of previous shell, ch 7, turn, shell in shell. Ch 3, sc in 8th dc of same dc group of flower, ch 3, turn, shell in shell, ch 7, turn, shell in shell. †*Ch 3, sc in 3rd dc of next dc group of flower, ch 3, turn, shell in shell, ch 7, turn, shell in shell. Ch 3, sc in 8th dc of same dc group, ch 3, turn, shell in shell, ch 7, turn, shell in shell.* Rep bet *s 3 times. (Ch 7, turn, shell in shell) twice. Ch 3, sc in 3rd dc of any dc group of a new flower, ch 3, turn, shell in shell, ch 3, work an sc inserting hook through the 3 previous ch-7 lps, ch 4, turn, shell in shell. Ch 3, sc in 8th dc of same dc group. Ch 3, turn, shell in shell, ch 3, dc in next free ch-7 sp. Ch 3, turn, shell in shell. Rep from † around, working in 6 dc groups of each flower after the first one. End by working into the first flower. Fasten off. Sew the ch-3 sp of the last shell to the beg ring. There will be 2 free dc groups on each flower. Weave in all ends.

CENTER

With white, ch 10, join with sl st in first ch to form ring.
Rnd 1: Work 16 sc in ring, join with sl st in first sc.
Rnd 2: Ch 6, dc in same st as sl st, *skip next sc, work dc, ch 3, dc in next sc; rep from * 6 times, join in 3rd ch of beg ch-6, sl st in next ch-3 sp—8 dc groups.
Rnd 3: Ch 3, work dc, ch 3, 2 dc in same sp, *work 2 dc, ch 3, 2 dc in next ch-3 sp; rep from * around, join in top of beg ch 3, sl st in next dc and ch-3 sp.
Rnd 4: Ch 3, work 2 dc, ch 3, 3 dc in same sp—first shell completed, dc bet the dc groups, *shell in next ch-3 sp, dc bet the dc groups; rep from * around, join in top of ch 3, sl st in each of next 2 dc and in next ch-3 sp.
Rnd 5: Ch 3, complete first shell, *skip 3 dc of shell, work dc, ch 3, dc in next dc, shell in ch-3 sp of next shell; rep from * around, end last rep with work dc, ch 3, dc in last dc, join in top of beg ch 3, sl st in each of next 2 dc and in ch-3 sp.

Rnd 6: Ch 3, complete first shell, *skip 3 dc of shell, dc in next dc, ch 5, dc in next dc, shell in next shell; rep from * around, end last rep with join in top of beg ch 3, sl st in each of next 2 dc and in next ch-3 sp.

Rnd 7: Ch 3, complete first shell, *skip 3 dc of shell, dc in next dc, ch 7, dc in next dc, shell in next shell; rep from * around, end last rep with join in top of beg ch 3, sl st in each of next 2 dc and in next ch-3 sp.

Rnd 8: Ch 3, complete first shell, *skip 3 dc of shell, dc in next dc, ch 9, dc in next dc, shell in next shell; rep from * around, end last rep with join in top of beg ch 3, sl st in each of next 2 dc and in next ch-3 sp.

Rnd 9: Ch 3, complete first shell, *skip 3 dc of shell, dc in next dc, ch 6, sc in ch-9 sp, ch 6, dc in next dc, shell in next shell; rep from * around, end last rep with join in top of beg ch 3, sl st in each of next 2 dc and in next ch-3 sp.

Rnd 10: Ch 3, work 2 dc, ch 3, 3 dc, ch 3, 3 dc in same sp, *skip 3 dc of shell, dc in next dc, ch 6, sc in next ch-6 sp, sc in next sc, sc in next ch-6 sp, ch 6, dc in next dc, work 3 dc, ch 3, 3 dc, ch 3, 3 dc all in next shell; rep from * around, end last rep with join in top of beg ch-3, sl st in each of next 2 dc and in next ch-3 sp.

Rnd 11: Ch 3, work 2 dc, ch 3, 3 dc in same sp to complete first shell, *ch 3, shell in next ch-3 sp, skip 3 dc, dc in next dc, ch 6, skip next ch-6 sp and sc, sc in next sc, ch 6, skip next sc and ch-6 sp, dc in next dc, shell in next ch-3 sp; rep from * around, end last rep with join in top of beg ch-3, sl st in each of next 2 dc and in next ch-3 sp.

Rnd 12: Ch 3, complete first shell, *ch 3, skip 3 dc, dc in next ch-3 sp, ch 3, shell in next shell, skip 3 dc, dc in next dc, ch 7, dc in next dc, shell in next shell; rep from * around, end last rep with join in top of beg ch-3, sl st in each of next 2 dc and in next ch-3 sp.

Rnd 13: Ch 3, complete first shell, *(ch 4, dc in next ch-3 sp) twice, ch 4, shell in next shell, skip 3 dc of shell, dc in next dc, ch 5, dc in next dc, shell in next shell; rep from * around, end last rep with join in top of beg ch-3, sl st in each of next 2 dc and in next ch-3 sp.

Rnd 14: Ch 3, complete first shell, *(ch 5, dc in next ch 4 sp) 3 times, ch 5, shell in next shell, skip 3 dc of shell, dc in next dc, ch 3, dc in next dc, shell in next shell; rep from * around, end last rep with join in top of beg ch-3, sl st in each of next 2 dc and in next ch-3 sp.

Rnd 15: Ch 3, complete first shell, *(ch 6, dc in next ch-5 sp) 4 times, ch 6, shell in next shell, skip 3 dc of shell, dc in each of next 2 dc, shell in next shell; rep from * around, end last rep with join in top of beg ch-3, sl st in each of next 2 dc and in next ch-3 sp.

Join center inside ring of flowers as follows: ch 3, 2 dc in same sp, *ch 5, dc in next ch-6 sp, ch 3, tr in the joined lp of edging to the left of the free lp of edging, ch 3, dc in next ch-6 sp of center, ch 3, sc bet 5th and 6th dc of first dc group of next flower, ch 3, 5 sc in next ch-6 sp of center, ch 3, sc bet 5th and 6th dc of next dc group of flower, ch 3, dc in next ch-6 sp of center, ch 3, tr in next joined lp of edging, ch 3, dc in next ch-6 sp of center, ch 5, 3 dc in next shell of center, sc in next free lp of edging, ch 3, 3 dc in next shell of edging. Rep from * around, ending with sl st at starting point. Fasten off. Weave in ends.

Filet Garden Runner

Size: Approximately 44" by 16".

MATERIALS

DMC Brilliant Knitting/Crochet Cotton—4 balls.
Size 8 steel crochet hook.

Gauge: 7 mesh = 2"; 7 rows = 2".

SPECIAL INSTRUCTIONS

Mesh: Ch 2, skip 2 sts or chs, dc in next st.
Block over block: Dc in each of next 3 sts.
Block over mesh: 2 dc in next ch-2 sp, dc in next dc.
Picot: Ch 4, sc in 3rd ch from hook, ch 1.
Cluster: (Yo hook and draw up a lp in sp, yo and draw through 2 lps) 3 times, yo and draw through all lps on hook.

Ch 153.

Row 1: Dc in 9th ch from hook and in each of next 6 chs, *ch 2, skip next 2 chs, dc in each of next 7 chs; rep from * across, end with ch 2, skip next 2 chs, dc in last ch.

Row 2: Ch 3, turn, 2 dc in first ch-2 sp, dc in each of next 4 dc—2 blocks made; work 45 mesh and 1 block, 2 dc in last ch-2 sp, skip 2 chs of turning ch, dc in next ch.

Row 3: Ch 3, turn, dc in each of next 3 dc to complete first block, work 1 mesh, 1 block, 43 mesh, 1 block, 1 mesh, 1 block.

Row 4: Ch 5, turn, skip first 3 dc, dc in next dc to complete first mesh, work 2 more mesh, 1 block, 5 mesh, 2 blocks, 13 mesh, 1 block, 13 mesh, 2 blocks, 5 mesh, 1 block, 3 mesh and 1 block.

Starting with Row 5, follow chart through Row 76, then work Rows 75 through 1 to complete the runner. Do not fasten off.

EDGING

Ch 3, (yo and draw up a lp in last mesh made, yo and through 2 lps) twice, yo and draw through all lps on hook—starting cluster made; *ch 3, sc bet the next 2 rows ending with blocks, ch 3, cluster in next mesh, work picot, cluster in same sp;* rep bet *s along long edge, ch 3, work cluster, picot, cluster, picot and cluster in corner mesh. Rep bet *s along short edge, working the sc in the dc at the center of the 2 blocks. Continue around in this manner, working cluster, picot, cluster, picot in last corner, join in top of first cluster. Fasten off. Weave in ends.

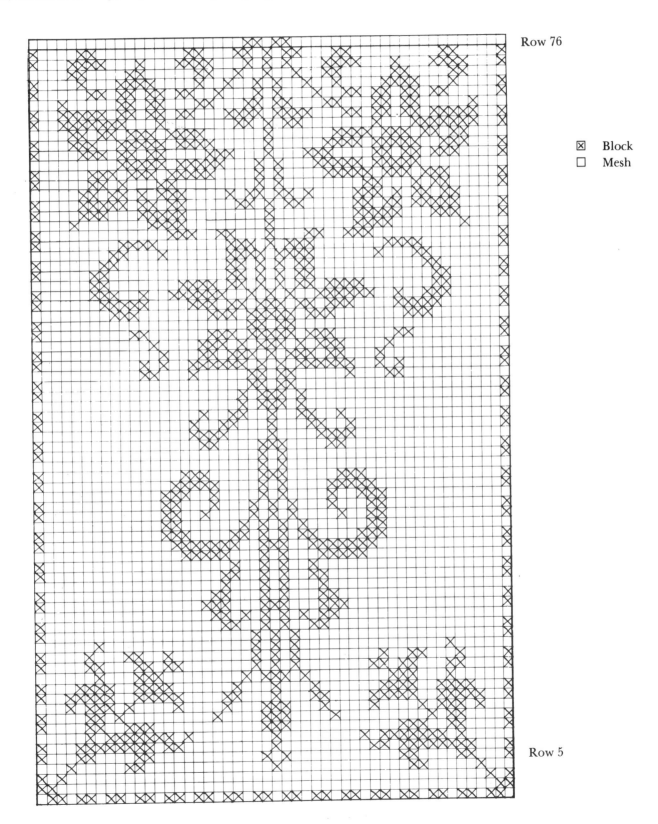

Row 76

☒ Block
☐ Mesh

Row 5

Filet Roses Centerpiece

Size: Approximately 23" by 14".

MATERIALS

DMC Cordonnet Special, size 40—3 balls.
Size 13 steel crochet hook.

Gauge: 7 mesh = 1"; 7 rows = 1".

SPECIAL INSTRUCTIONS

Mesh: Ch 2, skip 2 sts or chs, dc in next st.
Block over block: Dc in each of next 3 sts.
Block over mesh: 2 dc in ch-2 sp, dc in next dc.
Dec at beg of row: Turn work, work 3 sl sts in each block or mesh to be dec'd, sl st in first st of next block or mesh, ch 2 and complete row.
Dec at end of row: Do not work across sts to be dec'd.

The doily is made in two sections beginning with the center row.

FIRST HALF

Ch 300.
Row 1: Dc in 4th ch from hook and in each of next 3 chs—1 block made, ch 2, skip 2 chs, dc in next ch—1 mesh made; work 1 block, 2 mesh, 4 blocks, 1 mesh, 2 blocks, 1 mesh, 2 blocks, 8 mesh, 7 blocks, 20 mesh; mark last mesh worked for center, work 19 mesh, 7 blocks, 8 mesh, 2 blocks, 1 mesh, 2 blocks, 1 mesh, 4 blocks, 2 mesh, 1 block, 1 mesh and 1 block. Work last dc in top of beg ch.

Row 2: Ch 3, turn on this and every row. Follow the chart from the right-hand edge to the left-hand edge, then work back to the right-hand edge; do not repeat the center mesh.

Continue to follow the chart in this manner, dec'g as indicated, until Row 47 has been completed.

From this point on, the center motif is not symmetrical and is given in full on the chart.

Row 48: Follow the chart to the left-hand edge; then, skipping the stitches to the left of the heavy line, work back to the right-hand edge to complete the row.

Continue to follow the chart in this manner, dec'g as indicated, until Row 72 has been completed.

The remaining rows are given in full on the chart.

Row 73: Reading the chart from right to left, work across the row.

Row 74: Reading the chart from left to right, work across the row.

Continue in this manner, reading odd-numbered rows from right to left and even-numbered rows from left to right until the chart has been completed. Fasten off.

SECOND HALF

Turn the piece so that the center row is up and the end of the row is at the right. Attach the thread in the last stitch of the center row, ch 3. Beg with Row 2, work as for the first half. Fasten off and weave in all ends.

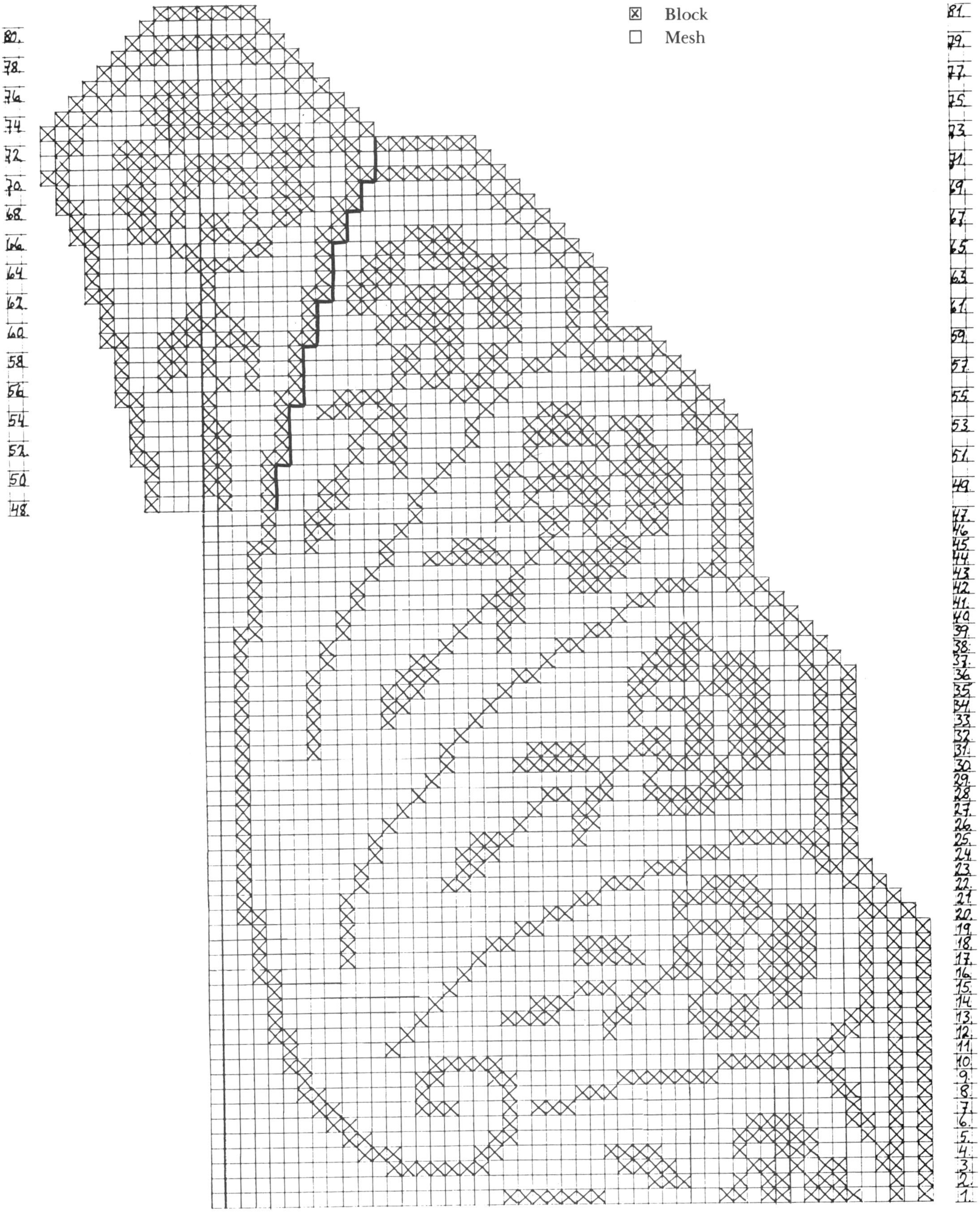
Block
Mesh

Trellis Runner

Size: *Approximately 18″ by 34″.*

MATERIALS

DMC Cebelia, size 30—3 balls.
Sizes 12 and 13 steel crochet hooks.

Gauge: 6 mesh = 1″; 6 rows = 1″

SPECIAL INSTRUCTIONS

Mesh: Ch 2, skip 2 sts or chs, dc in next st.
Block over block: Dc in each of next 3 sts.
Block over mesh: 2 dc in next ch-2 sp, dc in next dc.
Dec at beg of row: Turn work, work 3 sl sts in each block or mesh to be dec'd, sl st in first st of next block or mesh, ch 2 and complete row.
Dec at end of row: Do not work across sts to be dec'd.

The runner is made in 2 sections, beginning with the center row.

FIRST HALF

With size 13 hook, ch 330.
Center row: Following the chart, dc in 4th ch from hook and in each of next 3 chs—1 block made, ch 2, skip 2 chs, dc in next ch—1 mesh made; work 1 block, 5 mesh, 1 block, 9 mesh, (1 block, 7 mesh) 4 times, 1 block, 4 mesh.

Mark last mesh worked for center mesh. Work back to the right-hand edge of the chart as follows: 3 mesh, 1 block, (7 mesh, 1 block) 4 times, 9 mesh, 1 block, 5 mesh, 1 block, 1 mesh, 1 block. Work last dc in top of beg ch.
Row 1: Change to size 12 hook. Ch 3 and turn on this and every row. Following the chart, dc in each of next 3 sts to complete first block, work 1 mesh, 1 block, 5 mesh, 1 block, 8 mesh, 1 block, (1 mesh, 1 block, 5 mesh, 1 block) 4 times; work 1 mesh, 1 block, 3 mesh. Skip the center st on the chart and work back to the right-hand edge of the chart.
Row 2: Ch 3, turn; follow the chart from the right-hand edge to the left-hand edge, then work back to the right-hand edge. Do not rep the center st.
Rows 3–27: Follow the chart.
Next 16 rows: Rep Rows 12–27 of the chart.
 Continue to follow the chart, dec'g as indicated, until Row 86 has been completed; fasten off.

SECOND HALF

Turn the piece so that the center row is up and the end of the row is at the right. With the size 12 hook, attach the thread in the last st of the center row and ch 3. Beg with Row 1, work as for the first half of the runner. Fasten off and weave in all ends.

EDGING

Working along side edge, attach thread in top of center row, *ch 2, yo and draw up a lp in same sp, yo and draw through 1 lp, (yo and draw through 2 lps) twice, ch 2, sl st in next row;* rep bet *s along long edge, ending with sl st in top of Row 66 (last row before dec's). Ch 2, tr in same sp, ch 2, skip inner corner and sl st in top of next row. Continue working along edge, working each corner in this manner and ending with a sl st in top of Row 83.

Ch 2, yo and draw up a lp in same sp, yo and draw through 1 lp, (yo and draw through 2 lps) twice, ch 2, skip 2 sts, sl st in next st; ch 2, tr in same sp, ch 2, skip inner corner, sl st in top of next row; rep bet **s twice, ch 2, tr in same sp, ch 2, skip inner corner, sl st in top of next row; rep bet **s 3 times, ch 2, tr in same sp, ch 2, skip inner corner, sl st in top of last row. Rep bet **s across row. Work around rem edges to correspond. Fasten off. Weave in ends.

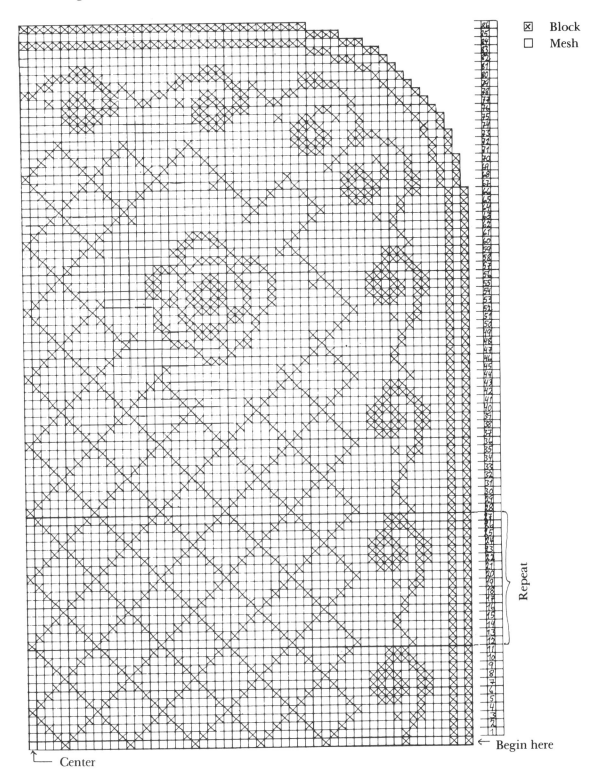

☒ Block
☐ Mesh

Repeat

← Begin here

└ Center

Glittering Star Tree Ornaments

MATERIALS

DMC gold embroidery thread #282 or silver embroidery thread #283—1 spool will make about 3 stars.
Size 10 steel crochet hook.

SPECIAL INSTRUCTIONS

Picot: Ch 3, sc in 3rd chain from hook.

Star #1 (far left)

Ch 10, join with sl st in first ch to form ring.
Rnd 1: Ch 3, work 23 dc in ring, join with sl st in top of beg ch 3.
Rnd 2: Ch 3, dc in same st, 2 dc in each of next 23 dc, join in top of beg ch 3.
Rnd 3: *Ch 3, skip next dc, sc in next dc; rep from * 22 times, ch 2, *dc* in base of beg ch 3—24 ch-sps.
Rnd 4: *(Ch 5, sc in next ch-5 sp) 4 times, ch 2, dc in next

ch-5 sp. Turn work. (Ch 5, sc in next ch-5 sp) 3 times, ch 2, dc in next ch-5 sp. Turn work. (Ch 5, sc in next ch-5 sp) 2 times, ch 2, dc in next ch-5 sp. Turn work. Ch 5, sc in next ch-5 sp, ch 2, dc in next ch-5 sp. Turn work. Ch 5, sc in next ch-5 sp. Fasten off. Attach thread in next free ch-5 sp of Rnd 3. Repeat from * 3 times; do not fasten off after 4th point.

Rnd 5: Ch 1, *working along side edge of point, (3 sc in next ch-sp, work picot) 4 times, 3 sc in next ch-sp, (3 sc in next ch-sp, work picot) 5 times, work 3 sc, picot, 3 sc, picot in sp at tip of point. Rep from * around, join in first sc. Fasten off. Weave in ends.

Star #2 (2nd from left)

Ch 6, join with sl st in first ch to form ring.

Rnd 1: Ch 10, (tr in ring, ch 7) 7 times, join with sl st in 3rd ch of beg ch 10.

Rnd 2: Ch 1, work 9 sc in each ch-7 sp, join in first sc.

Rnd 3: Ch 1, *sc in each of next 3 sc, 3 sc in next sc, sc in each of next 3 sc, skip 2 sc; rep from * around, join in first sc.

Rnd 4: Rep Rnd 3.

Rnd 5: Ch 3, *skip next sc, dc in next sc, ch 1, skip next sc, work dc, ch 2, tr, ch 2, and dc in next sc, ch 1, skip next sc, dc in next sc, skip next 2 sc, dc in next sc; rep from * around; join in top of beg ch 3.

Rnd 6: *Sc in next dc, sc in next ch-1 sp, sc in next dc, 2 sc in next ch-2 sp, 3 sc in next tr, 2 sc in next ch-2 sp, sc in next dc, sc in next ch-1 sp, sc in each of next 2 dc; rep from * around, join in first sc. Fasten off. Weave in ends.

Star #3 (center)

Ch 10, join with sl st in first ch to form ring.

Rnd 1: Ch 1, work 18 sc in ring.

Rnd 2: Sc in first sc of previous rnd, *ch 2, tr in same sc, ch 3, work 6 dc around tr just made, skip next 2 sc of ring, sc in next sc; rep from * around, end last rep with 6 dc around tr, join with sl st in first sc—6 leaves; sl st in each ch to tip of first leaf.

Rnd 3: *Sc in first dc on leaf, ch 3, sc in same st, ch 6; rep from * around on each leaf, end last rep with ch 6, join in first sc.

Rnd 4: *5 sc in next ch-3 sp, 10 sc in next ch-6 sp; rep from * around, join in first sc, sl st in each of next 2 sc.

Rnd 5: Ch 6, dc in same sp, *ch 1, skip next 3 sc, tr in each of next 8 sc, ch 1, skip next 3 sc, work dc, ch 3 and dc in next sc; rep from * around, end last rep with ch 1, join in 3rd ch of beg ch 6, sl st in next ch-sp.

Rnd 6: Ch 6, work dc, ch 3 and dc in same sp, *ch 3, skip next dc, ch-1 sp and 2 tr, sc in each of next 4 tr, ch 3, skip next 2 tr, ch-1 sp and dc, work dc, ch 3, dc, ch 3 and dc in next ch-sp; rep from * around, end last rep, sc in 4 tr, ch 3, join in 3rd ch of beg ch 6, sl st in next ch-sp.

Rnd 7: Ch 4, work picot, in same sp work dc, ch 1, picot, ch 1 and dc, *ch 3, skip next dc, in next sp work (dc, ch 1, picot, ch 1) twice, dc in same sp, ch 3, skip next ch-sp and 1 sc, sc in each of next 2 sc, ch 3, skip next sc and ch-sp, in next ch-sp work (dc, ch 1, picot, ch 1) twice, dc in same sp. Rep from * around, end last rep with sc in 2 sc, ch 3, join in 3rd ch of beg ch 4. Fasten off. Weave in ends.

Star #4 (2nd from right)

Ch 6, join with sl st in first ch to form ring.

Rnd 1: Ch 3, 15 dc in ring, join with sl st in top of beg ch 3.

Rnd 2: Ch 13, sc in same st as sl st, *sc in each of next 4 dc, ch 13, sc in same st as last sc; rep from * around, end with sc in each of last 3 sc, sl st in sl st.

Rnd 3: *(Sc in ch-13 lp, work picot) 9 times, sc in same lp, sc in each of next 5 sc of previous rnd; rep from * around, end last rep with sc in each of last 4 sc.

Rnd 4: *Ch 16, sc in 5th picot of next lp, ch 16, skip rem picots on lp and next 2 sc, sc in each of next 3 sc; rep from *, end last rep with sl st in each of last 3 sc of previous rnd.

Rnd 5: 20 sc in first ch-16 lp, *work sc, ch 4 and sc in next sc, 20 sc in next ch-16 lp, skip next sc, sl st in next sc, skip next sc, 5 sc in next ch-16 lp, remove lp from hook, insert hook in 15th sc of last ch-16 lp, pick up dropped lp and draw through, 15 sc in remainder of ch-16 lp; rep from * twice, 15 sc in last ch-16 lp, sl st in 5th sc of next lp, 5 sc in remainder of ch-16 lp. Fasten off.

Rnd 6: Attach thread in any ch-4 sp, *7 sc in ch-4 sp, work 6 picots, skip 20 sc, dc in joining of lps, work 6 picots; rep from * around, end with sl st in first sc. Fasten off. Weave in ends.

Star #5 (far right)

Ch 10, join with sl st in first ch to form ring.

Rnd 1: Ch 3, 29 dc in ring, join with sl st in top of beg ch 3.

Rnd 2: Ch 3, skip next 2 dc, dc in next dc, *ch 8, sc in 2nd ch from hook, hdc in each of next 2 chs, dc in each of next 2 chs, tr in each of next 2 chs, yo, draw up a lp in last dc worked in on ring, yo and draw through 2 lps, skip 2 dc on ring, yo and draw up a lp in next dc, yo and draw through 2 lps, yo and draw through all 3 lps on hook; rep from * around, end last rep with sc in top of beg ch 3—10 points.

Rnd 3: *Ch 7, sc in top of next point, ch 7, sc in st bet this point and next point; rep from * 8 times, ch 7, sc in top of next point, yo hook 6 times, draw up a lp in last sc of previous rnd, (yo and draw through 2 lps) 7 times.

Rnd 4: *Ch 9, sc in sc at top of next point, work 3 picots, sc in same sc; rep from * around. Fasten off. Weave in ends.

Filet Heart Table Runner

*Size: Approximately 45″ by 11¼″. Each motif
measures about 11¼″ square.*

MATERIALS

DMC Cordonnet Special, size 20—3 balls.
Size 12 steel crochet hook.

Gauge: 15 mesh = 4″; 15 rows = 4″.

SPECIAL INSTRUCTIONS

Mesh: Ch 2, skip 2 sts or chs, tr in next st.
Block over block: Tr in each of next 3 sts.
Block over mesh: 2 tr in next ch-2 sp, tr in next tr.
Picot: Ch 4, sl st in 4th ch from hook.

FIRST MOTIF

HEART BLOCK

Ch 58.
Row 1: Tr in 10th ch from hook, *ch 2, skip next 2 chs, tr in next ch; rep from * across—17 mesh.
Row 2: Ch 6, turn on this and every row, skip first tr and ch-sp, tr in next tr, *ch 2, skip next ch-sp, tr in next tr; rep from * 14 times, ch 2, skip 2 chs of turning ch, tr in next ch.
Row 3: Ch 6, turn, skip first tr and ch-sp, tr in next tr, ch 2, skip next ch-sp, tr in next tr, *2 tr in next ch-sp, tr in

next tr; rep from * 12 times, ch 2, skip next ch-sp, tr in next tr, ch 2, skip 2 chs of turning ch, tr in next ch.

Starting with Row 4, follow chart through Row 17. Fasten off.

EDGING

Rnd 1: Join thread in any corner mesh, ch 5, 15 dtr in same mesh, *(ch 2, skip next mesh, 4 tr in next mesh) 7 times, ch 2, skip next mesh, work 16 dtr in corner mesh; rep from * twice, (ch 2, skip next mesh, 4 tr in next mesh) 7 times, ch 2, join in top of beg ch 5.

Rnd 2: Ch 6, (dtr in next dtr, ch 1) 14 times, dtr in next dtr, †*ch 2, skip next ch-2 sp and 3 tr, (tr in next tr, 2 tr in next ch-2 sp, tr in next tr, ch 2, skip next 2 tr) 5 times, ch 2, skip next 2 tr, tr in next tr, 2 tr in next ch-2 sp, tr in next tr, ch 2, skip next 3 tr and ch-2 sp,* (dtr in next dtr, ch 1) 15 times, dtr in next dtr; rep from † twice, rep bet *s once more, join in 5th ch of beg ch 6.

Rnd 3: Ch 7, (dtr in next dtr, ch 2) 14 times, dtr in next dtr, †*ch 2, skip next ch-2 sp and 3 tr, (tr in next tr, 2 tr in next ch-2 sp, tr in next tr, ch 2, skip next 2 tr) 4 times, ch 2, skip next 2 tr, tr in next tr, 2 tr in next ch-2 sp, tr in next tr, ch 2, skip next 3 tr and ch-2 sp,* (dtr in next dtr, ch 2) 15 times, dtr in next dtr; rep from † twice, rep bet *s once more, join in 5th ch of beg ch 7.

Rnd 4: Ch 8, (dtr in next dtr, ch 3) 14 times, dtr in next dtr, †*ch 2, skip next ch-2 sp and 3 tr, (tr in next tr, 2 tr in next ch-2 sp, tr in next tr, ch 2, skip next 2 tr) 3 times, ch 2, skip next 2 tr, tr in next tr, 2 tr in next ch-2 sp, tr in next tr, ch 2, skip next 3 tr and ch-2 sp,* (dtr in next dtr, ch 3) 15 times, dtr in next dtr; rep from † twice, rep bet *s once more, join in 5th ch of beg ch 8.

Rnd 5: Ch 9, (dtr in next dtr, ch 4) 14 times, dtr in next dtr, †*ch 2, skip next ch-2 sp and 3 tr, (tr in next tr, 2 tr in next ch-2 sp, tr in next tr, ch 2, skip next 2 tr) 2 times, ch 2, skip next 2 tr, tr in next tr, 2 tr in next ch-2 sp, tr in next tr, ch 2, skip next 3 tr and ch-2 sp,* (dtr in next dtr, ch 4) 15 times, dtr in next dtr; rep from † twice, rep bet *s once more, join in 5th ch of beg ch 9.

Rnd 6: Ch 10, (dtr in next dtr, ch 5) 14 times, dtr in next dtr, †*ch 2, skip next ch-2 sp and 3 tr, tr in next tr, 2 tr in next ch-2 sp, tr in next tr, ch 2, skip next 2 tr, tr in next tr, 2 tr in next ch-2 sp, tr in next tr, ch 2, skip next 3 tr and ch-2 sp,* (dtr in next dtr, ch 5) 15 times, dtr in next dtr; rep from † twice, rep bet *s once more, join in 5th ch of beg ch 10.

Rnd 7: Ch 11, (dtr in next dtr, ch 6) 14 times, dtr in next dtr, †*ch 2, skip next ch-2 sp and 3 tr, tr in next tr, 2 tr in next ch-2 sp, tr in next tr, ch 2, skip next 2 tr, tr in next tr, 2 tr in next ch-2 sp, tr in next tr, ch 2, skip next 3 tr and ch-2 sp,* (dtr in next dtr, ch 6) 15 times, dtr in next dtr; rep from † twice, rep bet *s once more, join in 5th ch of beg ch 11.

Rnd 8: Ch 9, work picot, ch 4, †*(dtr in next dtr, ch 4, work picot, ch 4) 14 times, dtr in next dtr,* ch 4, sl st bet 2nd and 3rd tr of next tr group, ch 4,* (dtr in next dtr, ch 4, work picot, ch 4) 15 times, dtr in next dtr; rep from † twice, rep bet *s once more, join in 5th ch of beg ch 9. Fasten off. Weave in ends.

SECOND MOTIF

Word as for first motif through Rnd 7 of Edging.

Rnd 8: Ch 9, work picot, ch 4, (dtr in next dtr, ch 4, work picot, ch 4) 9 times, *dtr in next dtr, ch 4, dc in corresponding picot of first motif, ch 4, dtr in next dtr, ch 4, sc in corresponding picot of first motif, ch 4, dtr in next dtr, ch 4, dc in corresponding picot of first motif,* (ch 4, dtr in next dtr, ch 4, work picot, ch 4) twice, dtr in next dtr, ch 4, sl st bet 2nd and 3rd tr of next tr group, ch 4, (dtr in next dtr, ch 4, work picot, ch 4) twice; rep bet *s once; complete rnd as for first motif.

Make two more motifs, joining them as before to make a strip.

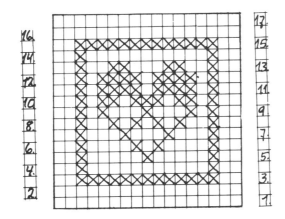

☒	Block
☐	Mesh

Rose Motif Bedspread

*Size: Approximately 60" by 85". Each motif
measures about 8½" square.*

MATERIALS

DMC Brilliant Knitting/Crochet Cotton—24 balls ecru,
6 balls green ombré #92.
Size 1 steel crochet hook.

Gauge: Block should measure approximately 2" across
from sc to sc after Rnd 8.

SPECIAL INSTRUCTIONS

Picot: Ch 4, sl st in last st made.
Sc-dec: Insert hook through front lp of first sc and
through back lp of next sc, yo and draw up a lp, yo and
draw through both lps on hook.

FIRST BLOCK

With ecru, ch 4, join with sl st in first ch to form ring.
Rnd 1: Ch 1, 8 sc in ring, join in first sc.
Rnd 2: Ch 1, sc in same sp, *ch 3, sc in next sc; rep from * 7
times, ch 3, join at base of beg ch 3. Fasten off.
Rnd 3: With green, sc in any sc, *5 dc in next ch-3 sp, sc in
next sc; rep from * around, end last rep with join in first
sc—8 petals.
Rnd 4: Ch 1, sc in same sp, *holding petals forward so
that the chain passes behind them, ch 3, sc in next sc; rep
from * around, end last rep with join in first sc.
Rnd 5: Ch 1, sc in same sp, *7 dc in next ch-3 sp, sc in next
sc; rep from * around, end last rep with join in first sc.
Rnd 6: Ch 1, sc in same sp, *holding petals forward so
that the chain passes behind them, ch 3, sc in next sc; rep
from * around, end last rep with join in first sc.
Rnd 7: Ch 1, sc in same sp, *9 dc in next ch-3 sp, sc in next
sc; rep from * around, end last rep with join in first sc.
Fasten off.
Rnd 8: With ecru, sc in any sc, *holding petals forward so
that the chain passes behind them, ch 3, sc in next sc; rep
from * around, end last rep with join in first sc.
Rnd 9: Ch 4, work dc, ch 1 and dc all in same sp as last sl
st, *ch 5, skip 9 dc, work dc, ch 1, dc, ch 1 and dc all in
next sc; rep from * around, end ch 5, join in 3rd ch of beg
ch 4—8 dc groups.
Rnd 10: Ch 8, *dc in last dc of same group, ch 5, dc in first
dc of next group, ch 5; rep from * around, end last rep
with ch 5, join in 3rd ch of beg ch 8.
Rnd 11: Ch 1, sc in same sp, *ch 3, work dc, ch 5 and dc in
next ch-sp, ch 3, sc in next dc, 6 sc in next ch-sp, sc in next
dc, 5 sc in next ch-sp, sc in next dc, 6 sc in next ch-sp, sc in
next dc; rep from * 3 times, end last rep with join in first
sc.

Rnd 12: *Ch 3, skip next ch-3 sp, 9 dc in next ch-5 sp for corner, ch 3, skip next ch-3 sp, work sc-dec over next 2 sc, sc in each of next 17 sc, work sc-dec over next 2 sc; rep from * around, working last sc-dec over last sc of Rnd 11 and joining sl st.

Rnd 13: *Ch 3, skip next ch-3 sp, dc in next dc, (ch 1, dc in next dc) 8 times, ch 3, skip next ch-3 sp, work sc-dec over next 2 sc, sc in each of next 15 sc, work sc-dec over next 2 sc; rep from * around.

Rnd 14: *Ch 3, skip ch-3 sp and dc, (2 dc in next ch-1 sp, ch 1) 7 times, 2 dc in next ch-1 sp, ch 3, skip next ch-3 sp, work sc-dec over next 2 sc, sc in each of next 13 sc, work sc-dec over next 2 sc; rep from * around.

Rnd 15: *Ch 3, skip next ch-3 sp, sc in next dc, (ch 3, sc in next ch-1 sp) 7 times, ch 3, skip next dc, dc in next dc, ch 3, skip next ch-3 sp, work sc-dec over next 2 sc, sc in each of next 11 sc, work sc-dec over next 2 sc; rep from * around.

Rnd 16: *Ch 3, skip next ch-3 sp and sc, 3 dc in next ch-3 sp, (ch 3, 3 dc in next ch-3 sp) 8 times, ch 3, skip next ch-3 sp, work sc-dec over next 2 sc, sc in each of next 9 sc, work sc-dec over next 2 sc; rep from * around.

Rnd 17: *Ch 3, skip next ch-3 sp, sc in next dc, (ch 5, sc in next ch-1 sp) 7 times, ch 5, skip next 2 dc, sc in next dc, ch 3, skip next ch-3 sp, work sc-dec over next 2 sc, sc in each of next 7 sc, work sc-dec over next 2 sc; rep from * around.

Rnd 18: *Ch 3, skip next ch-3 sp and sc, 5 dc in next ch-5 sp, (ch 1, 5 dc in next ch-5 sp) 7 times, ch 3, skip next ch-3 sp, work sc-dec over next 2 sc, sc in each of next 5 sc, work sc-dec over next 2 sc; rep from * around.

Rnd 19: *Ch 3, skip next ch-3 sp, sc in next dc, ch 3, skip next dc, (dc in next dc, ch 3, skip next 2 dc, sc in next ch-1 sp, ch 3, skip next 2 dc) 7 times, dc in next dc, ch 3, skip next 2 dc, sc in next sc, ch 3, skip next ch-3 sp, work sc-dec over next 2 sc, sc in each of next 3 sc, work sc-dec over next 2 sc; rep from * around.

Rnd 20: *Ch 3, skip next ch-3 sp, sc in next sc, (ch 4, dc in next dc, work picot, ch 4, sc in next sc) 8 times, ch 3, skip next ch-3 sp, work sc-dec over next 2 sc, sc in next sc, work sc-dec over next 2 sc; rep from * around, end with sl st in base of first ch 3. Fasten off.

SECOND BLOCK

Work as for first block through Rnd 19.

Rnd 20: Begin as for first block, working instructions within the parentheses a total of 5 times—5 picots made. *Ch 4, dc in next dc, ch 2, remove hook from lp and insert it in corresponding picot of first block, pick up dropped lp and draw thread through picot, ch 2, sl st in last dc made, ch 4, sc in next sc;* rep bet *s once, ch 4, dc in next dc, work picot, ch 4, sc in next sc, ch 3, skip next ch-3 sp, sc-dec over next 2 sc, sc in next sc, ch 4, dc in next dc, ch 1. Yo hook 5 times; from wrong side, draw up a lp in last picot made, (yo and draw through 2 lps) twice—5 loops on hook. Yo twice and draw up a lp in corresponding picot of finished block (last picot of last corner), (yo and draw through 2 lps) twice—6 lps on hook. Yo twice, draw up a lp in next picot of finished block (first picot of next corner), (yo and draw through 2 lps) twice—7 lps on hook. Yo and draw through 4 lps, (yo and draw through 2 lps) 3 times, ch 2, sl st in last dc made, ch 4, sc in next sc. Rep bet *s twice;† complete rnd as for first block.

THIRD BLOCK

Work as for second block, joining it to the adjacent side of the first block (*Fig. 1*).

FOURTH BLOCK

Work as for second block through †, joining it to the adjacent edge of the second block to form a square (*Fig. 2*). Work corner as follows: Ch 4, dc in next dc, work picot, ch 4, sc in next sc, ch 4, dc in next dc, ch 1. Yo hook 7 times; from wrong side, draw up a lp in last picot made, (yo and draw through 2 lps) 3 times—6 lps on hook. Yo hook 3 times, draw up a lp in the first free picot of the block to the right, (yo and draw through 2 lps) 3 times—7 lps on hook. Yo 3 times; draw up a lp in next free picot of same block, (yo and draw through 2 lps) 3 times—8 lps on hook. Yo 3 times and draw up a lp in first free picot of next block, (yo and draw through 2 lps) 3 times—9 lps on hook. Yo 3 times and draw up a lp in next free picot of same block, (yo and draw through 2 lps) 3 times—10 lps on hook. Yo 3 times and draw up a lp in first free picot of last block, (yo and draw through 2 lps) 3 times—11 lps on hook. Yo 3 times and draw up a lp in next free picot of same block, (yo and draw through 2 lps) 3 times—12 lps on hook. Yo and draw through 7 lps, (yo and draw through 2 lps) 5 times, sl st in last dc made, ch 4, sc in next sc. Continue around, joining second side to adjacent motif.

Continue to make and join blocks in this manner until you have 70 blocks joined in 10 rows of 7 blocks each. Weave in ends.

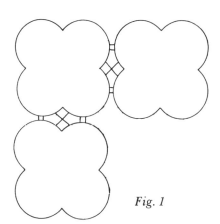

Fig. 1

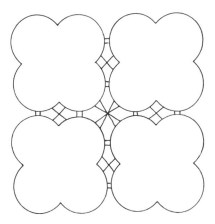

Fig. 2

Classic Filet Luncheon Set

*Sizes: Runner, approximately 37½" by 10";
placemat, approximately 19½" by 14";
doily, approximately 6" square.*

MATERIALS

DMC Cebelia, size 30—3 balls for runner, 2 balls for placemat and 1 ball for doily. 3 balls will make the entire set.

Size 13 steel crochet hook.

Gauge: 7 mesh = 1"; 5 rows = 1".

SPECIAL INSTRUCTIONS

Mesh: Ch 2, skip 2 sts or chs, dc in next st.
Double mesh: Ch 5, skip 2 blocks or mesh (or 1 double mesh), dc in next dc.
2 single mesh over 1 double mesh: Ch 2, dc in ch-5 sp, ch 2, dc in next dc.
Block over block: Dc in each of next 3 sts.
Block over mesh: 2 dc in ch-2 sp, dc in next dc.
Cluster: (Yo and insert hook in 2nd st of ch-2 sp, draw up a lp to dc height) 4 times, yo and draw through all lps on hook, dc in next dc.
2 clusters over 1 double mesh: Cluster in 2nd ch of ch-5, dc in next ch, cluster in 5th ch, dc in next dc.

Placemat

Ch 328.
Row 1: Dc in 5th ch from hook and in each rem ch—325 dc, counting beg ch 4.
Row 2: Ch 3, turn on this and every row; dc in each of next 6 dc—2 blocks made, ch 2, skip 2 sts, dc in next st—1 mesh made; *work (2 blocks, 2 mesh) 25 times, work 2 blocks, 1 mesh, 2 blocks. Work last dc in top of beg ch.
Row 3: Ch 3, turn, dc in each of next 3 sts to complete first block; work 1 mesh, 1 block, (2 mesh, 2 blocks) 25 times, 2 mesh, 1 block, 1 mesh, 1 block. Work last dc in top of beg ch.
Rows 4 and 5: Ch 3, turn, dc in each of next 6 sts, work 104 mesh, 2 blocks.
Row 6: Reading Row 6 of Chart I from right to left, first work section A, then work section B 4 times; complete the row by working section C.

Work each row in the same manner, working double mesh and clusters as indicated, until Row 41 of the chart has been completed. Repeat Rows 6–41 once, then repeat Rows 6–24 once more. Work Rows 42–46 to complete the placemat. Fasten off. Weave in ends.

Runner

Ch 628.

Row 1: Dc in 5th ch from hook and in each rem ch—625 sts, counting beg ch-4.

Rows 2 and 3: Work as for Rows 2 and 3 of placemat, working the instructions within the parentheses 50 times in all.

Rows 4 and 5: Ch 3, turn, dc in each of next 6 sts, work 204 mesh, 2 blocks.

Beg with Row 6 and reading chart from right to left, follow Chart I as for placemat, repeating section B 9 times on each row.

Doily

Ch 100.

Row 1: Dc in 5th ch from hook and in each rem ch—97 sts, counting beg ch 4.

Rows 2 and 3: Work as for placemat, working instructions within parentheses 6 times in all.

Beg with Row 4 and reading chart from right to left, follow Chart II through Row 22, then work Rows 22 through 1. Fasten off. Weave in ends.

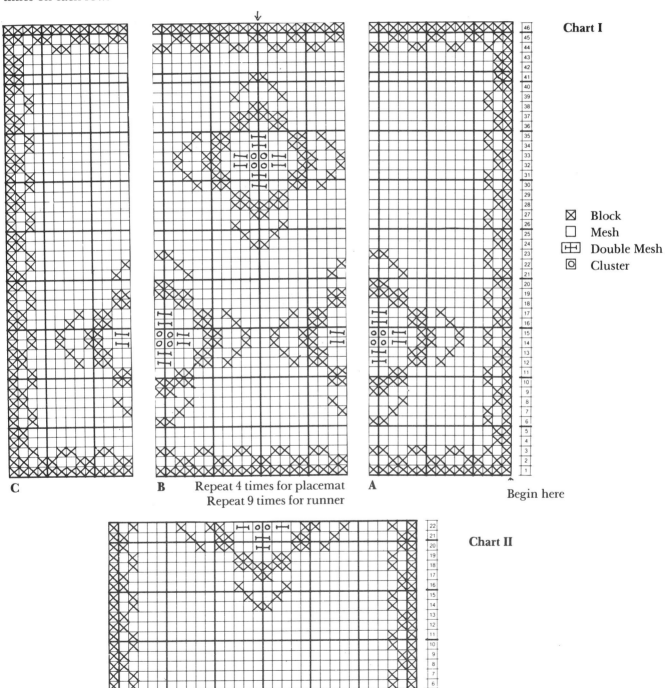

Chart I

⊠ Block
☐ Mesh
⊞ Double Mesh
⊡ Cluster

C

B Repeat 4 times for placemat
Repeat 9 times for runner

A

Begin here

Chart II

Begin here

39

Lucky Clover Table Runner and Napkin

Size: Table runner, approximately 29″ by 17″; napkin, approximately 7″ square.

MATERIALS

DMC Cordonnet Special, size 20—3 balls white.
DMC Pearl Cotton, size 8—4 balls green ombré.
Size 12 steel crochet hook.

Gauge: Each motif measures approximately 5¼″ square.

SPECIAL INSTRUCTIONS

Picot: Ch 3, sc in first ch made.

Motif

FIRST HEART-SHAPED LEAF

With green, ch 17.
Row 1: Dc in 8th st from hook, *ch 2, skip next 2 chs, dc in next ch; rep from * 3 times—4 ch-sps.
Row 2: Turn, ch 5, skip first dc and ch-sp, *dc in next dc, ch 2; rep from * twice, skip 2 sts of turning ch, dc in next ch.

Rows 3 and 4: Rep Row 2.

Row 5: Do not turn work. Working along side edge, ch 1, 3 sc in first sp, *3 sc in next sp, ch 5, 3 sc in next sp,* 7 sc in corner sp; rep bet *s along next edge, 3 sc in next sp.

Rnd 6: Turn work; in first ch-5 sp work (ch 1, dtr) 11 times, skip next 6 sc, sc in corner sc, skip next 6 sc, work (dtr, ch 1) 11 times in next ch-5 sp, skip next 6 sc, sl st in next sc, work picot, 3 sc in each of next 2 ch-sps along next edge, work picot, 3 sc in next ch-sp, work 3 sc, picot and 3 sc in corner ch-sp, 3 sc in next ch-sp, work picot, 3 sc in each of last 2 ch-sps, (sc in next ch-1 sp, sc in next dtr) 11 times, sc in next sc, (sc in next sc, sc in next ch-1 sp) 11 times, sl st in next sl st. Fasten off. Weave in ends.

SECOND LEAF

Work as for first leaf through Rnd 5.

Rnd 6: Turn work; in first ch-5 sp, work (ch 1, dtr) 11 times, skip next 6 sc, sc in corner sc, skip next 6 sc, (dtr, ch 1) 11 times in next ch-5 sp, skip next 6 sc, sl st in next sc, *ch 1, sl st in corresponding picot of first leaf, ch 1, sc in first ch made,* 3 sc in each of next 2 ch-sps, rep bet *s, 3 sc in each of next 2 ch-sps; rep bet *s, 3 sc in same ch-sp, complete rnd as for first leaf.

Make 2 more leaves, joining them to the first 2 leaves as before to form a square.

Rnd 7: With right side of work facing, join white with sl st in 8th sc from end of any leaf. Ch 3, dc in each of last 7 sc of this leaf, *dc in each of first 5 sc of next leaf, remove hook from lp, skip 10 dc to the right and insert hook in next dc (this will be the 5th dc from the end of the previous leaf), pick up dropped lp, yo and draw thread through lp and stitch to join leaves, dc in each rem sc of leaf; rep from * around, join with sl st in top of beg ch 3.

Rnd 8: Ch 3, skip next 2 dc of this leaf, skip joining st and next 2 dc of next leaf, tr in next dc, *(ch 6, skip next 2 dc, sc in next dc) 9 times, ch 6, skip next 2 dc, yo twice and draw up a lp in next st, (yo and draw through 2 lps) twice, skip next 2 dc of this leaf, joining st and next 2 dc of next leaf; yo twice and draw up a lp in next st, (yo and draw through 2 lps) twice, yo and draw through all 3 lps on hook; rep from * around, end last rep with ch 3, tr in first tr to bring the thread into position for the next rnd.

Rnd 9: *Ch 6, sc in next ch-sp; rep from * around, end last rep with ch 3, tr in last tr of Rnd 8.

Rnd 10: *(Ch 6, sc in next ch-sp) 5 times, ch 5, work 3 tr, ch 5 and 3 tr all in next sp, ch 5, sc in next ch-sp, (ch 6, sc in next ch-sp) 3 times; rep from * around, end last rep with ch 2, dtr in last tr of Rnd 9.

Rnd 11: Ch 3, 2 dc around dtr just made, *(ch 3, 3 dc in next ch-sp) 4 times, ch 3, work 3 tr, ch 5 and 3 tr all in next ch-sp, tr in next ch-sp, work 3 tr, ch 13 and 3 tr all in next ch-sp for corner, tr in next ch-sp, work 3 tr, ch 5 and 3 tr all in next ch-sp, (ch 3, 3 dc in next ch-sp) twice; rep from * around, end last rep with ch 3, sl st in top of beg ch 3.

Runner

Work first motif as above. Work a second motif through Rnd 10.

Rnd 11: Ch 3, 2 dc around dtr just made, *(ch 3, 3 dc in next ch-sp) 4 times, ch 3, work 3 tr, ch 5 and 3 tr all in next ch-sp, tr in next ch-sp, 3 tr in next sp, ch 6, sl st in corresponding sp of previous motif, ch 6, 3 tr in same sp as last 3 tr, tr in next ch-sp, 3 tr in next ch-sp, ch 2, sl st in corner sp of previous motif, ch 2, 3 tr in same sp as last 3 tr, (ch 1, sl st in corresponding sp of previous motif, ch 1, 3 dc in next sp of second motif) 6 times, ch 1, sl st in first motif, ch 1, 3 tr in next ch-sp, ch 2, sl st in first motif, ch 2, 3 tr in same sp as last 3 tr, tr in next sp, 3 tr in next sp, ch 6, sl st in first motif, ch 6, 3 tr in same sp as last 3 tr; complete second motif as for first.

Make 15 motifs, joining them in 5 rows of 3 motifs each.

EDGING

Rnd 1: Join white with sl st in any corner, ch 8, (dc in same sp, ch 5) 3 times, †*skip 3 tr, tr in next tr, (ch 5, sc in next ch-sp) 9 times, ch 5, skip next 3 tr, tr in next tr, ch 5, dc in next ch-sp, ch 5, dc in joining of motifs, ch 5, dc in next ch-sp, ch 5.* Rep bet *s along edge. After last tr before corner, work (ch 5, dc in corner sp) 4 times, ch 5. Rep from † around, end after last tr with ch 5, join in 3rd ch of beg ch 8.

Rnd 2: Ch 3, *5 dc in next ch-sp, dc in next st; rep from * around, end with 5 dc in last ch-sp, join in 3rd ch of beg ch 8.

Rnd 3: Ch 1, sc in same sp, *work 3 picots, skip next 5 dc, sc in next dc; rep from * around, end last rep with sl st in first sc. Fasten off, weave in ends.

Napkin

Work 1 motif as above.

EDGING

Rnd 1: Join white with sl st in any corner, ch 8, (dc in same sp, ch 5) 3 times, *skip next 3 tr, tr in next tr, (ch 5, sc in next ch-sp) 9 times, ch 5, skip 3 tr, tr in next tr, ch 5, (dc in corner sp, ch 5) 4 times; rep from * around, end after last tr with ch 5, join in 3rd ch of beg ch 8.

Rnds 2 and 3: Rep Rnds 2 and 3 of runner.

Mitered Filet Centerpiece

Size: Approximately 32" square.

MATERIALS

DMC Brilliant Knitting/Crochet Cotton—5 balls.
Size 5 steel crochet hook.

Gauge: 3 mesh = 1"; 3 rows = 1".

SPECIAL INSTRUCTIONS

Mesh: Ch 2, skip 2 sts or chs, dc in next st.
Block over block: Dc in each of next 3 sts.
Block over mesh: 2 dc in ch-2 sp, dc in next dc.
Picot: Ch 4, sc in 3rd ch from hook, ch 1.
Cluster: (Yo hook and draw up a lp, yo and draw through 2 lps) 3 times—4 lps on hook. Yo and draw through all lps.
Shell: 3 dc, ch 4, 3 dc all in same sp.

The centerpiece is worked in rnds following the chart. Rnd 1 is shown in its entirety; one quarter of each rem rnd is shown.

Ch 8, join with sl st in 1st ch to form ring.

Rnd 1: Ch 3, 3 dc in ring, *(ch 4 for corner, 4 dc in ring) 3 times, ch 4 for last corner, join in top of beg ch 3.

Rnd 2: Beg at arrow on chart, ch 5, skip next 2 dc, dc in next dc—1 mesh made, *shell in corner mesh, dc in next dc, ch 2, skip next 2 dc, dc in next dc;* rep bet *s twice, shell in last corner mesh, join in 3rd ch of beg ch 5.

Rnd 3: Ch 5, dc in next dc, ch 2, skip 2 dc, dc in next dc, *shell in corner mesh, dc in next dc, ch 2, skip next 2 dc, dc in next dc, ch 2, skip next sp, dc in next dc, ch 2, skip next 2 dc, dc in next dc; rep from * twice, shell in last corner mesh, dc in next dc, ch 2, join in 3rd ch of beg ch 5.

Rnd 4: Following chart, ch 5, dc in next dc to complete first mesh, work 2 more mesh, *shell in corner mesh, dc in next dc, turn chart 90° to the right and work 3 mesh as on chart. Turn chart back to the left and, beg with the mesh to the left of the heavy line on the chart, work 2 more mesh. Rep from * around, end last rep with join in 3rd ch of beg ch 5.

Rnd 5: Ch 5 and complete first mesh, work 3 more mesh, *shell in corner, dc in next dc; turn chart 90° and work 4 mesh as on chart; turn chart back to the left and, beg with the mesh to the left of the heavy line, work 4 mesh. Rep from * around, end last rep with join in 3rd ch of beg ch 5.

Rnd 6: Ch 3, 2 dc in next ch-2 sp, dc in next dc to complete first block, work 4 mesh, *shell in corner, dc in next dc; turn chart, work 4 mesh, 1 block; turn chart back, work 4 mesh; rep from *around, end with join in top of beg ch 3.

Continue to follow the chart through Rnd 44.

Rnd 45: Ch 1, sl st back to the right in the previous mesh, ch 1, sc in same sp, *ch 4, skip next mesh, (cluster in next mesh, work picot) 4 times, cluster in next mesh, ch 4, skip next mesh, sc in next mesh;* rep bet *s 4 times, **ch 4, skip next mesh, cluster in next mesh, work picot, cluster in next mesh, work picot, skip next block, in corner mesh work (cluster, picot) 4 times, skip next block, cluster in next mesh, work picot, cluster in next mesh, ch 4, skip next mesh, sc in next mesh.** Rep from * along each edge, working from ** to ** at each corner; end with join in first sc. Fasten off. Weave in ends.

Center

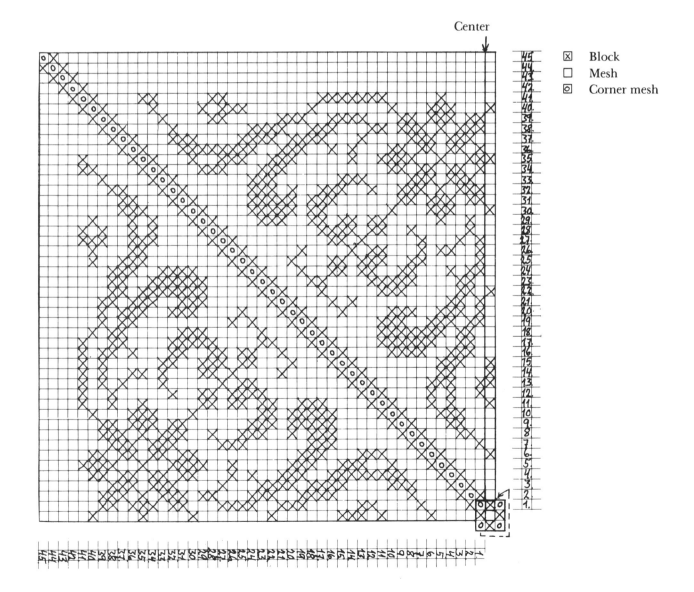

☒	Block
☐	Mesh
◉	Corner mesh

Snowflake Table Runner

Size: Approximately 42" by 11".

MATERIALS

DMC Cordonnet Special, size 10—4 balls
Size 10 steel crochet hook.

Gauge: Each small snowflake measures approximately 3¾" in diameter.

SPECIAL INSTRUCTIONS

Picot: Ch 3, dc in 3rd ch from hook.
Picot group: Dc in sp, ch 1, work picot, ch 1.

The table runner is made up of 4 motifs, each consisting of 7 flowers.

FIRST SNOWFLAKE

Ch 10, join with sl st in first ch to form ring.
Rnd 1: 18 sc in ring.
Rnd 2: Sc in first sc of previous rnd, *ch 2, tr in same sc, ch 3, work 6 dc around tr just made, skip next 2 sc of ring, sc in next sc; rep from * around, end last rep with join in first sc, sl st in next 2 chs and in next tr—6 points.

Rnd 3: Sc in first dc of point, *ch 3, sc in same dc, ch 6, sc in first dc of next point; rep from * around, end last rep with join in first sc.
Rnd 4: *5 sc in next ch-3 sp, 10 sc in next ch-6 sp; rep from * around, end last rep with join in first sc, sl st in each of next 2 sc.
Rnd 5: Ch 6, dc in same sc as last sl st, *ch 1, skip next 3 sc, tr in each of next 8 sc, ch 1, skip next 3 sc, work dc, ch 3 and dc in next sc; rep from * around, end last rep with join in 3rd ch of beg ch 6, sl st in next ch-3 sp.
Rnd 6: Ch 6, dc in same sp, ch 3, dc in same sp, *ch 3, skip next dc, ch-1 sp and 2 tr, sc in each of next 4 tr, ch 3, skip next 2 tr, ch-1 sp and dc, work dc, ch 3, dc, ch 3 and dc in next ch-3 sp; rep from *, end last rep with join in 3rd ch of beg ch 6, sl st in next ch-3 sp.
Rnd 7: Ch 4, work picot, ch 1, work picot group and dc in same sp, †*ch 3, work 2 picot groups and 1 dc in next ch-3 sp, ch 3, skip next dc, ch-3 sp and sc, sc in each of next 2 sc, ch 3, skip next sc, ch-3 sp and dc,* work 2 picot groups and 1 dc in next ch-3 sp; rep from † 4 times, then rep bet *s once more, join in 3rd ch of beg ch 6. Fasten off. Weave in ends.

SECOND SNOWFLAKE

Work as for first snowflake through Rnd 6.

Rnd 7: Begin as for first snowflake, repeating from † 3 times instead of 4, ch 3, dc in next ch-3 sp, *(ch 2, sc in corresponding picot of previous snowflake, ch 1, skip 1 ch, sc just made and 1 ch, dc in next ch to complete picot, ch 1, dc in same sp) twice,* ch 3, skip next dc, ch-3 sp and sc, sc in each of next 2 sc, ch 3, skip next sc, ch-3 sp and dc, dc in next ch-3 sp; rep bet *s once, dc in same sp, complete rnd as for first snowflake.

Make and join a total of 6 snowflakes to form a ring, leaving 2 picots free on each snowflake on the inner edge of the ring. The 6th snowflake should be joined to both the first and the 5th snowflake. Make a 7th snowflake for the center of the ring, joining it to all of the free picots. This completes one motif.

Make 3 more motifs in the same way, joining them as in the photograph.

Lace Medallion Tablecloth

Size: *Approximately 75" in diameter.*

MATERIALS

DMC Brilliant Knitting/Crochet Cotton—18 balls.
Size 4 steel crochet hook.

Gauge: Center motif should measure approximately 5½" after Rnd 8.

SPECIAL INSTRUCTIONS

Picot: Ch 6, insert hook in upper lp at side of last dc made and draw up a lp; to work next dc, yo and draw up a lp in sp, yo and draw through 2 lps, yo and draw through 3 lps.
Shell: Work sc, hdc, 3 dc, picot, 3 dc, hdc and sc all in same sp.

Petal: *Yo twice, draw up a lp in sp, (yo and draw through 2 lps) twice; rep from * 3 times—5 lps on hook; yo and draw through 4 lps, yo and draw through 2 lps.
3-Petal group: *Yo twice and draw up a lp in sp, (yo and draw through 2 lps) twice;* rep bet *s twice—4 lps on hook, yo and draw through 3 lps, yo and draw through 2 lps; ch 3, sc in same sp, ch 3; rep bet *s twice—3 lps on hook, (yo and draw through 2 lps) twice; ch 3, sc in same sp, ch 3; rep bet *s 3 times—4 lps on hook, yo and draw through 3 lps, yo and draw through 2 lps.
Reverse petal cluster: Ch 4, in last sc (or sl st) made, **yo twice and draw up a lp, (yo and draw through 2 lps) twice;** rep bet **s twice—4 lps on hook, yo and draw through 3 lps, yo and draw through 2 lps. Ch 5, insert hook in 2 upper lps at side of petal just made and draw up

a lp, skip next ch-2 sp, dc and ch-2 sp. Rep bet **s 4 times in next dc—6 lps on hook, yo and draw through 5 lps, yo and draw through 2 lps. Ch 4; working in 2 upper lps of petal just made, rep bet **s 3 times—4 lps on hook, yo and draw through 3 lps, yo and draw through 2 lps. Skip next ch-2 sp, dc and ch-2 sp, sc in next dc.

V-st: Work dc, ch 3 and dc all in same sp.

CENTER

Ch 8, join with sl st in first ch to form ring.

Rnd 1: Ch 1, work 15 sc in ring, join with sl st in beg ch 1.

Rnd 2: Ch 7, *skip next st, dc in next st, ch 4; rep from * 6 times, join with sl st in 3rd ch of beg ch 7—8 ch sps.

Rnd 3: Work sc, hdc, 3 dc, hdc and sc in each ch-sp around; sl st in first sc and in next hdc.

Rnd 4: *Ch 5, skip next 3 dc, sc in next hdc, ch 5, skip next 2 sts, sc in next hdc; rep from * around, end last rep with ch 3, dc in sl st at base of beg ch 5 to bring thread into position for next rnd.

Rnd 5: Ch 3, sc around dc just made, *ch 5, work sc, ch 3 and sc in next ch-5 sp; rep from * around, end with ch 3, dc in upper lp of dc of 4th rnd.

Rnd 6: Ch 3, sc around dc just made, *ch 5, skip next sc, ch 3 and sc, work sc, ch 3 and sc in next ch-5 sp; rep from * around, end with ch 3, dc in upper lp of dc of previous rnd.

Rnd 7: Ch 4, sc around dc just made, *ch 6, skip next sc, ch 3 and sc, work sc, ch 4 and sc in next ch-5 sp; rep from * around, end with ch 4, dc in lower lp of dc of previous rnd.

Rnd 8: *Ch 7, skip next sc, ch 4 and sc, sc in next ch-6 sp; rep from * around, end with sl st in top of dc of previous rnd—16 ch-sps.

Rnd 9: Work sc, hdc, 9 dc, hdc and sc in each ch-sp; sl st in back lp of each of first 7 sts of rnd.

Rnd 10: Sc in same st as last sl st, *ch 11, sc in the side of the sc just made to form a ring, ch 9, skip next 12 sts, sc in next st; rep from * around; end after last ring with ch 6, dc at base of first ring.

Rnd 11: *Work 23 dc in next ring, work sc, ch 4 and sc in next ch-6 sp; rep from * around, end with sl st in back lp of each of first 10 dc of first ring.

Rnd 12: *Ch 5, skip next 3 sts, sc in next st, ch 5, skip 3 sts, **yo twice, pick up a lp in next st, yo and draw through 2 lps, yo and draw up a lp in 6th dc of next ring, (yo and draw through 2 lps) 4 times,** (ch 5, skip 2 sts, sc in next st) 3 times, ch 5, skip next 2 sts, rep bet **s, ch 5, skip next 3 sts, sc in next st. Rep from * around, end after last joined st with ch 3, dc in sl st at base of beg ch 5.

Rnd 13: *Ch 6, skip next st, sc in next ch-sp; rep from * around, end with ch 3, dc in dc at end of previous rnd—56 ch-sps.

Rnd 14: Rep Rnd 13.

Rnd 15: *Ch 6, skip next st, sc in next ch-sp; rep from * around, end with ch 6, sc in same ch-sp as last sc, ch 3, dc in dc at end of previous rnd—57 ch-sps.

Rnds 16–18: Rep Rnd 13.

Rnd 19: *Ch 6, skip next st, sc in next ch-sp, skip next st, work 5 dc, ch 3, 5 dc in next ch-sp, skip next st, sc in next ch-sp; rep from * around, end after last dc group with sc in next ch-sp, sl st in each of first 4 chs of beg ch 6.

Rnd 20: *Ch 5, work 3-petal group in ch-3 sp of next dc group, ch 5, sc in next ch-6 sp; rep from * around, end

after last 3-petal group with ch 5, sl st in sl st at base of beg ch 5 and in each of first 3 chs.

Rnd 21: *Ch 6, sc in the ch-3 sp at the right-hand side of the center petal of the next group, ch 6, sc in the ch-3 sp at the left-hand side of the same petal, (ch 6, sc in the next ch-5 sp), twice; rep from * around, end with sl st in sl st at base of beg ch 6, sl st in each of first 3 chs.

Rnd 22: *Ch 6, sc in ch-sp above center petal, ch 6, sc in next ch-sp, work 5 dc, ch 5, 5 dc in next ch-sp; rep from * around, end with sl st in sl st at base of beg ch 6, sl st in each of first 3 chs.

Rnd 23: *Ch 6, sc in next ch-sp, ch 5, work 3-petal group in ch-5 sp of next dc group, ch 5, sc in next ch-sp; rep from * around, end after last 3-petal group with ch 5, sl st in sl st at base of beg ch 6, sl st in each of first 3 chs.

Rnd 24: *Ch 6, sc in next ch-sp, ch 6, sc in tip of center petal of next 3-petal group, (ch 6, sc in next ch-sp) twice; rep from * around, end with sl st in sl st at base of beg ch-6, sl st in each of first 3 chs.

Rnds 25–28: *Ch 6, sc in next ch-sp; rep from * around, end with sl st in sl st at base of beg ch 6, sl st in each of first 4 chs—76 ch-sps.

Rnds 29 and 30: *Ch 7, sc in next ch-sp; rep from * around, end with sl st in sl st at base of beg ch 6, sl st in each of first 4 chs.

Rnd 31: *Ch 7, sc in next ch-sp; rep from * around, end with sl st in sl st at base of beg ch 6.

Rnd 32: Work sc, hdc, 3 dc, picot, 3 dc, hdc and sc in each ch-sp; join in first sc. Fasten off.

Rnd 33: Join thread in any picot, sc in same sp, *ch 7, sc in next picot; rep from * around, end last rep with join in first sc.

Rnd 34: Ch 3, *6 dc in next ch-7 sp, dc in next sc; rep from * around, end last rep with join in top of beg ch 3.

Rnd 35: Ch 5, *dc bet 2nd and 3rd dc of next 6 dc group, ch 2, dc bet 4th and 5th dc of same group, ch 2, dc in dc above picot, ch 2; rep from * around, end last rep with ch 2, join in 3rd ch of beg ch 5.

Rnd 36: *Work reverse petal cluster over next 4 ch-sps; rep from * around, end with sc at base of beg ch 4, sl st in each of next 4 chs—57 clusters.

Rnd 37: Sc in ch-sp above center petal of cluster, ch 4, *yo twice and draw up a lp in same sp, (yo and draw through 2 lps) twice;* rep bet *s twice, yo and draw through 3 lps, yo and draw through 2 lps, **(ch 6, work leaf in same sp) twice, work leaf in ch-sp above center petal of next cluster; rep from ** around, end with sl st at top of first leaf, sl st in each of first 2 chs of next ch-6.

Rnd 38: Ch 5, *skip 2 chs, dc in next ch, ch 2, skip next ch, leaf and ch, dc in next ch, ch 2; rep from * around, end last rep with ch 2, skip next ch, leaf and ch, join in 3rd ch of beg ch 5.

Rnd 39: Ch 3, *2 dc in next ch-sp, dc in next dc; rep from * around, end last rep with join in top of beg ch 3.

Rnd 40: Ch 6, dc in same st as sl st, *ch 2, skip next 2 dc, in next dc, ch 2, skip next 2 dc, work V-st in next dc; rep from * around, end after last sc with ch 2, sl st in 3rd ch of beg ch 6, sl st in next ch-sp.

Rnd 41: Ch 6, dc in same sp, *ch 3, skip next sp, sc and ch-sp, work V-st in ch-3 sp of next V-st; rep from * around, end with ch 3, join in 3rd ch of beg ch 6.

Rnd 42: Ch 6, dc in same sp, *ch 2, sc in next ch-sp, ch 2, work V-st in next V-st; rep from * around, end with ch 2, join in 3rd ch of beg ch 6, sl st in next ch-sp—114 V-sts.

Rnds 43–47: Rep Rnds 41 and 42 alternately.

Rnd 48: Ch 6, dc in same sp, (ch 2, sc in next ch-sp, ch 2, work V-st in next V-st) 7 times, ch 2, sc in next ch-sp, ch 2, work dc, ch 3, dc, ch 3 and dc in next V-st, (ch 2, sc in next ch-sp, ch 2, work V-st in next V-st) 8 times, ch 2, sc in next ch-sp, ch 2, work dc, ch 3, dc, ch 3 and dc in next V-st, *(ch 2, sc in next ch-sp, ch 2, work V-st in next V-st) 7 times, ch 2, sc in next ch-sp, ch 2, work dc, ch 3, dc, ch 3 and dc in next V-st; rep from * around, end after last sc with ch 2, join in 3rd ch of beg ch 6, sl st in next ch-sp.

Rnd 49: Ch 6, dc in same sp, (ch 3, skip next ch-sp, sc and ch-sp, work V-st in next V-st) 7 times, ch 3, skip next ch-sp, sc and ch sp, work V-st in next ch-3 sp, ch 3, work V-st in next ch-3 sp, (ch 3, skip next ch-sp, sc and ch-sp, work V-st in next V-st) 8 times, ch 2, skip next ch-sp, sc and ch-sp, work V-st in next ch-3 sp, ch 3, work V-st in next ch-3 sp, *(ch 3, skip next ch-sp, sc and ch-sp, work V-st in next V-st) 7 times, ch 2, skip next ch-sp, sc and ch-sp, work V-st in next ch-3 sp, ch 3, work V-st in next ch-3 sp; rep from * around, end with ch 3, join in 3rd ch of beg ch 6, sl st in next ch-sp.

Rnd 50: Rep Rnd 42—128 V-sts.

Rnds 51 and 52: Rep Rnds 41 and 42.

Rnd 53: Sc in same sp as last sl st, ch 7, *skip next ch-sp, sc and ch-sp, sc in next V-st, ch 7; rep from * around, join in first sc. Fasten off. Weave in ends.

SMALL SIDE MEDALLIONS

Ch 6, join with sl st to form ring.

Rnd 1: Ch 6, *dc in ring, ch 3; rep from * 3 times, join with sl st in 3rd ch of beg ch 6—5 ch-sps.

Rnd 2: Work sc, hdc, 4 dc, hdc and sc in each ch-sp; sl st in each of first 3 sts.

Rnd 3: *Ch 5, skip next 3 dc, sc in next st, ch 5, skip next 3 sts, sc in next st; rep from * around, end last rep with ch 3, dc in sl st at base of beg ch 5.

Rnd 4: Ch 3, sc around dc just made, *ch 5, work sc, ch 4 and sc in next ch-sp; rep from * around, end with ch 3, dc in dc of previous rnd.

Rnd 5: Ch 3, sc around dc just made, *ch 5, skip next sc, ch-4 sp and sc, work sc, ch 4 and sc in next ch-5 sp; rep from * around, end with ch 3, dc in dc of previous rnd.

Rnd 6: Ch 3, sc around dc just made, *ch 6, skip next sc, ch-4 sp and sc, work sc, ch 4 and sc in next ch-5 sp; rep from * around, end with ch 3, dc in dc of previous rnd.

Rnd 7: Ch 8, sc in upper lp of dc just made, *ch 9, skip next sc, ch-4 sp and sc, sc in next ch-6 sp, ch 8, sc in side of sc just made to form ring; rep from * around, end after last ring with ch 6, dc in dc of previous rnd—10 rings.

Rnd 8: *Work 18 dc in next ring, sc, ch 4 and sc in ch-9 sp; rep from * around, end with sl st in back lp of each of first 8 dc of first ring.

Rnd 9: *Ch 5, skip next 2 sts, sc in next st, ch 5, yo twice, skip next 3 sts, pick up a lp in next st, yo and draw through 2 lps, yo, pick up a lp in 4th dc of next ring, (yo and draw through 2 lps) 4 times, ch 5, skip next 3 sts, sc in next dc; rep from *, end after last joined st with ch 3, dc in sl st at base of beg ch 5.

Rnd 10: *Ch 6, sc in next ch-sp; rep from * around, end with ch 3, dc in dc of previous rnd—30 ch-sps.

Rnds 11–13: Rep Rnd 10.

Rnd 14: *Ch 7, sc in next ch-sp; rep from * around, end with ch 7, sl st in dc of previous rnd.

Rnd 15: Work a shell in each ch-sp around, working the picots as follows: *First 3 ch-sps;* regular ch-6 picot. *4th ch-sp;* ch 25 for the picot instead of 6. *5th ch-sp;* ch 8, remove hook and insert it through the 13th ch of the last picot, pick up dropped lp and draw it through ch, ch 8, complete picot. *6th ch-sp;* ch 12, remove hook and insert it through the 13th ch of the 25-ch picot, pick up dropped lp and draw it through, ch 12, complete picot and shell. *7th and 8th ch-sps;* regular ch-6 picot. *9th, 10th and 11th ch-sps;* rep 4th, 5th and 6th picots. *12th, 13th, 14th, 15th and 16th ch-sps;* regular ch-6 picot. *17th, 18th and 19th ch-sps;* rep 4th, 5th and 6th shells. *20th and 21st ch-sps;* regular ch-6 picot. *22nd, 23rd and 24th ch-sps;* rep 4th, 5th and 6th shells. *25th, 26th and 27th ch-sps;* regular ch-6 picot. Do not work in the last 3 ch-sps of the motif. Do not fasten off, but cut thread, leaving about 1½ to 2 yds of thread to complete the medallion.

Work a second medallion through Rnd 14.

Rnd 15: Work first 16 ch-sps as for first motif. *17th ch-sp;* ch 12, draw the lp through 13th ch of 9th picot of previous medallion, ch 12, complete the picot. *18th ch-sp;* ch 8, join to 13th ch of 9th picot of previous medallion as before, ch 8, complete picot. *19th ch-sp;* ch 6, drop lp and insert hook through 7th and 19th ch of 9th picot of previous medallion and draw lp through, ch 6 and complete picot. *20th ch-sp;* ch 3, draw lp through 8th picot of previous medallion, ch 3 and complete picot. *21st ch-sp;* ch 3, draw lp through 7th picot of previous medallion, ch 3 and complete picot. *22nd ch-sp;* ch 6, draw lp through 6th ch of both sides of 6th picot of previous medallion, ch 3 and complete the picot. *23rd ch-sp;* ch 8, draw through 13th ch of 4th picot of previous medallion, ch 8 and complete picot. *24th ch-sp;* ch 12, draw through 13th ch of 4th picot of previous medallion, ch 12 and complete picot. Complete rnd as for first medallion.

Make and join a total of 16 medallions, working last rnd of last medallion as follows: Work first 3 ch-sps as for first medallion. *4th ch-sp;* ch 12, draw lp through joining of 22nd picot of first medallion, ch 12 and complete picot. *5th ch-sp;* ch 8, join in same place as last picot, ch 8 and complete picot. *6th ch-sp;* ch 6, draw lp through 7th and 19th ch of 22nd picot of first medallion, ch 6 and complete picot. *7th ch-sp;* ch 3, join in picot of 21st ch-sp of first medallion, ch 3 and complete picot. *8th ch-sp;* ch 6, join in 20th picot of first medallion, ch 6 and complete picot. *9th ch-sp;* ch 6, join in the 6th ch of both sides of 19th picot of first medallion, ch 6 and complete picot. *10th ch-sp;* ch 8, join in joining of 19th, 18th and 17th picots of first medallion, ch 8 and complete picot. *11th ch-sp;* ch 12, join in same place as last picot, ch 12 and complete picot. Complete medallion as for second medallion.

To join center to small side medallions, attach thread to any ch-7 sp on edge of center. Work a shell in each ch-7 sp, working picots as follows: *First ch-sp;* ch 3, join to picot at center of the 5 free picots on one small side medallion, ch 3 and complete picot. *2nd ch-sp;* ch 3, join in next picot of same medallion, ch 3 and complete picot. *3rd ch-sp;* ch 3, join in next picot of same medallion, ch 3 and complete picot. *4th ch-sp;* ch 6, draw lp through center of both sides of next picot of same medallion, ch 6 and complete picot. *5th ch-sp;* regular ch-6 picot with no joinings. *6th ch-sp;* ch 6, draw lp through center of both sides of next picot on next medallion, ch 6 and complete picot. *7th ch-sp;* ch 3, join in first free picot of same medallion, ch 3 and complete picot. *8th ch-sp;* ch 3, join in next free picot of same medallion, ch 3 and complete picot. Rep from * around, end with sl st in first sc. Fasten off.

LARGE SIDE MEDALLIONS

Ch 6, join with sl st in first ch to form ring.
Rnd 1: Ch 6, *dc in ring, ch 3; rep from * 4 times, join with sl st in 3rd ch of beg ch 6—6 ch-sps.
Rnd 2: Work sc, hdc, 4 dc, hdc and sc in each ch-sp; sl st in each of first 3 sts.
Rnd 3: *Ch 5, skip next 3 dc, sc in next st, ch 5, skip next 3 sts, sc in next st; rep from * around, end last rep with ch 3, dc in sl st at base of beg ch 5.
Rnd 4: Ch 3, sc around dc just made, *ch 5, work sc, ch 4 and sc in next ch-sp; rep from * around, end with ch 3, dc in dc of previous rnd.
Rnd 5: Ch 3, sc around dc just made, *ch 5, skip next sc, ch-4 sp and sc, work sc, ch 4 and sc in next ch-5 sp; rep from * around, end with ch 3, dc in dc of previous rnd.
Rnd 6: Ch 3, sc around dc just made, *ch 6, skip next sc, ch-4 sp and sc, work sc, ch 4 and sc in next ch-5 sp; rep from * around, end with ch 3, dc in dc of previous rnd.
Rnd 7: Ch 11, sc in upper lp of last dc made, *ch 9, skip next sc, ch-4 sp and sc, sc in next ch-sp, ch 11, sl st in side of last sc made to form ring; rep from * around, end after last ring with ch 6, dc in dc of previous ring—12 rings.
Rnd 8: *Work 24 dc in ring, sc, ch 4 and sc in next ch-9 sp; rep from * around, sl st in back lp of each of first 11 dc of ring.
Rnd 9: *Ch 5, skip 2 sts, sc in next st, ch 5, skip next 3 sts, **yo twice, pick up a lp in next st, yo and draw through 2 lps, yo and pick up a lp in 7th dc of next ring, (yo and draw through 2 lps) 4 times,** ch 5, skip 3 sts, sc in next st, ch 5, skip next 2 sts, sc in next st, ch 5, skip next 3 sts; rep bet **s once, (ch 5, skip next 2 sts, sc in next st) 3 times, ch 5, skip next 2 sts; rep bet **s once, ch 5, skip next 3 sts, sc in next st; rep from * around, end after last joined st with ch 3, dc in sl st at base of beg ch 5—40 ch-sps.
Rnds 10 and 11: *Ch 6, sc in next ch-sp; rep from * around, end ch 3, dc in last dc of previous rnd.
Rnd 12: *Ch 6, sc in next ch-sp, work 4 dc, ch 3, 4 dc in next ch-sp, sc in next ch-sp, (ch 6, sc in next ch-sp) twice; rep from * around, end with ch 3, dc in last dc of previous rnd—8 dc groups.
Rnd 13: *Ch 6, sc in next ch-sp, ch 5, work 3-petal group in ch-3 sp of next dc-group, ch 5, sc in next ch-sp, ch 6, sc in next ch-sp; rep from * around, end after last 3-petal group with ch 5, sc in next ch-sp, ch 3, dc in last dc of previous rnd.
Rnd 14: *Ch 6, sc in next ch-6 sp, ch 6, sc in next ch-5 sp, ch 6, sc in tip of center petal, ch 6, sc in next ch-5 sp, ch 6, sc in next ch-6 sp; rep from * around, end last rep with sc in next ch-5 sp, ch 3, dc in last dc of previous rnd.
Rnd 15: *Ch 6, sc in next ch-sp; rep from * around, end with ch 3, dc in last dc of previous rnd.
Rnd 16: *Ch 6, sc in next ch-sp; rep from * around, end with ch 6, sl st in last dc of previous rnd. Fasten off.

Rnd 17: Join thread with sl st at beg of last worked ch-sp. Work a shell in each ch-sp, working picots as follows: *First 25 ch-sps;* regular ch-6 picot. *26th, 27th and 28th ch-sps;* work as for 4th, 5th and 6th ch-sps of first small side medallion. *29th ch-sp;* ch 3, join to 27th picot of any small side medallion, ch 3 and complete picot. *30th ch-sp;* ch 3, join to 26th picot of small medallion, ch 3 and complete picot. *31st ch-sp;* ch 3, join to 25th picot of small medallion, ch 3 and complete picot. *32nd ch-sp;* ch 6, draw lp through 6th ch of both sides of 24th picot of small medallion, ch 6 and complete picot. *33rd ch-sp;* regular ch-6 picot with no joinings. *34th ch-sp;* ch 6, draw lp through center ch of both sides of 4th picot of next small medallion to the left, ch 6 and complete picot. *35th ch-sp;* ch 3, join to 3rd picot of same medallion, ch 3 and complete picot. *36th ch-sp;* ch 3, join to 2nd picot of same medallion, ch 3 and complete picot. *37th ch-sp;* ch 3, join to first picot of same medallion, ch 3 and complete picot. *38th, 39th and 40th ch-sps;* work as for 4th, 5th and 6th ch-sps of small medallion. End with sl st in first sc of rnd. Fasten off. Weave in ends.

Make a second medallion through Rnd 16.
Rnd 17: Join thread with sl st at right-hand edge of last worked ch-sp. *First ch-sp;* ch 3, join to 25th picot of previous large medallion, ch 3 and complete picot. *2nd ch-sp;* ch 3, join to 24th picot of previous large medallion, ch 3 and complete picot. *3rd ch-sp;* ch 3, join to 23rd picot of previous large medallion, ch 3 and complete picot. Work as for previous medallion through 37th ch-sp. *38th ch-sp;* ch 12, join to corresponding joining of previous medallion, ch 12 and complete picot. *39th ch-sp;* ch 8, join in same sp, ch 8 and complete picot. *40th ch-sp;* ch 6, join in center ch of both sides of corresponding picot of previous medallion, ch 6 and complete picot. End with sl st in first sc of rnd. Fasten off.

Make and join a total of 16 large medallions, working last rnd of last medallion as follows: Work 22 ch-sps as for previous medallion. *23rd ch-sp;* ch 3, join to 3rd picot of first medallion, ch 3 and complete picot. *24th ch-sp;* ch 3, join to 2nd picot of first medallion, ch 3 and complete picot. *25th ch-sp;* ch 3, join to first picot of first medallion, ch 3 and complete picot. *26th ch-sp;* ch 6, join in the center chs of both sides of the corresponding picot of the first medallion. *27th ch-sp;* ch 8, join in same place as last join, ch 8 and complete picot. *28th ch-sp;* ch 12, join in same place, ch 12 and complete medallion. Finish rnd as for second medallion.

To join small medallions to large medallions, finish each small medallion as follows: *28th ch-sp;* ch 6, join in center ch of both sides of picot-chs below, ch 6 and complete picot. *29th ch-sp;* regular ch-6 picot with no joinings. *30th ch-sp;* work as for 28th ch-sp. End with sl st in first sc of rnd. Fasten off. Weave in all ends.

FRINGE

Cut strands 14″ long. Holding 12 strands together, fold in half. Insert lp through center of joining of medallions, bring ends through lp and tighten. Rep in sp to either side of center. Continue to work 3 fringes bet each pair of medallions.